DESIGN ANARCHY

KALLE LASN

 ADBUSTERS

As a child I played in the gaps between buildings, ruins of buildings, fallow land, abandoned industrial areas, gravel pits and sand mines. Formed through misplanning, they were our empire, the empire of children.

Ours was a dirty, unused place, with snakes, lizards, insects of every category and wild vegetation.

Children instinctively understand the language of natural vegetation. They can read it, if only they're allowed to climb the fence and play undisturbed.

But the city gardeners arrive – the eliminators of mystery, the killers of the empty spaces. They mow, pave and plant in zones where children and teenagers once played.

They pave the paths people may walk upon and prohibit walking on the grass. The grass is always framed with perfectly composed borders and the flowers are always placed in identical pots of cement.

Naturalness is understood as the annihilation of spontaneity through perfect gardening.

AuTuM

my concern is
with the rythms
of nature
— POLLOCK

In the struggle between
commerce and culture,
commerce has triumphed
and the war is over.
— *Milton Glaser*

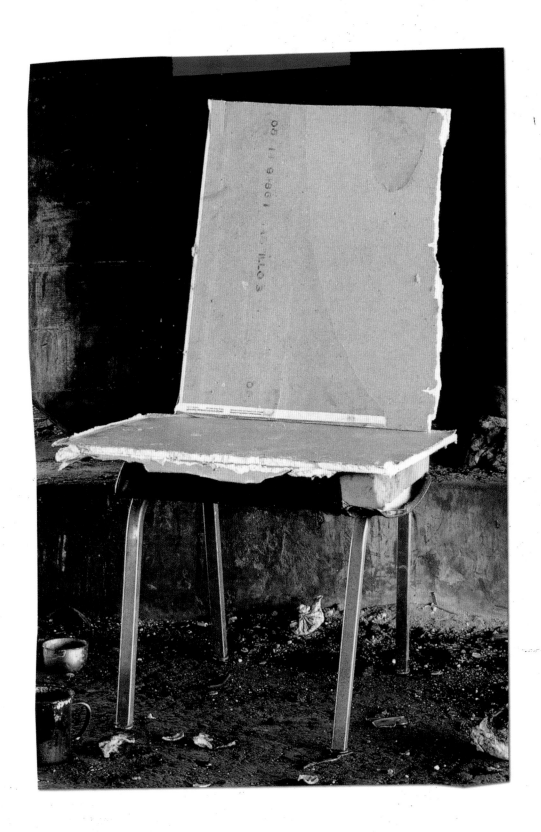

OURS...to fight for

Norman Rockwell

FREEDOM FROM WANT

1942

AMERICA: OPEN FOR BUSINESS

Following the September 11 attacks, San Francisco launched "America: Open for Business" – a campaign designed, in the words of Mayor Willie L. Brown Jr., to "let the world know this city, and this country, will rise from the ashes of the national tragedy." The idea was soon picked up by businesses and cities across the United States.

2001

I am so sick of the design scene – the art stars, the gravity-bending techno-prowess, the insatiable dissimulation of form and function.

I am sick of the endless competitions, the must-go pat-on-the-back conferences, the slick publications full of trivial show-and-tells.

I am sick of the Appolonian pixel-pushers, the corporate ass kissers, the self-annointed arbiters of good taste.

What design needs
is ten years
of total turmoil...
fuck-it-all anarchy...
after that maybe it will
mean something again...
stand for
something again...

TAKE ALL KEEP ALL.
MY SOUL WALKS WITH ME.
FORM OF FORMS.

CHAPTER 0

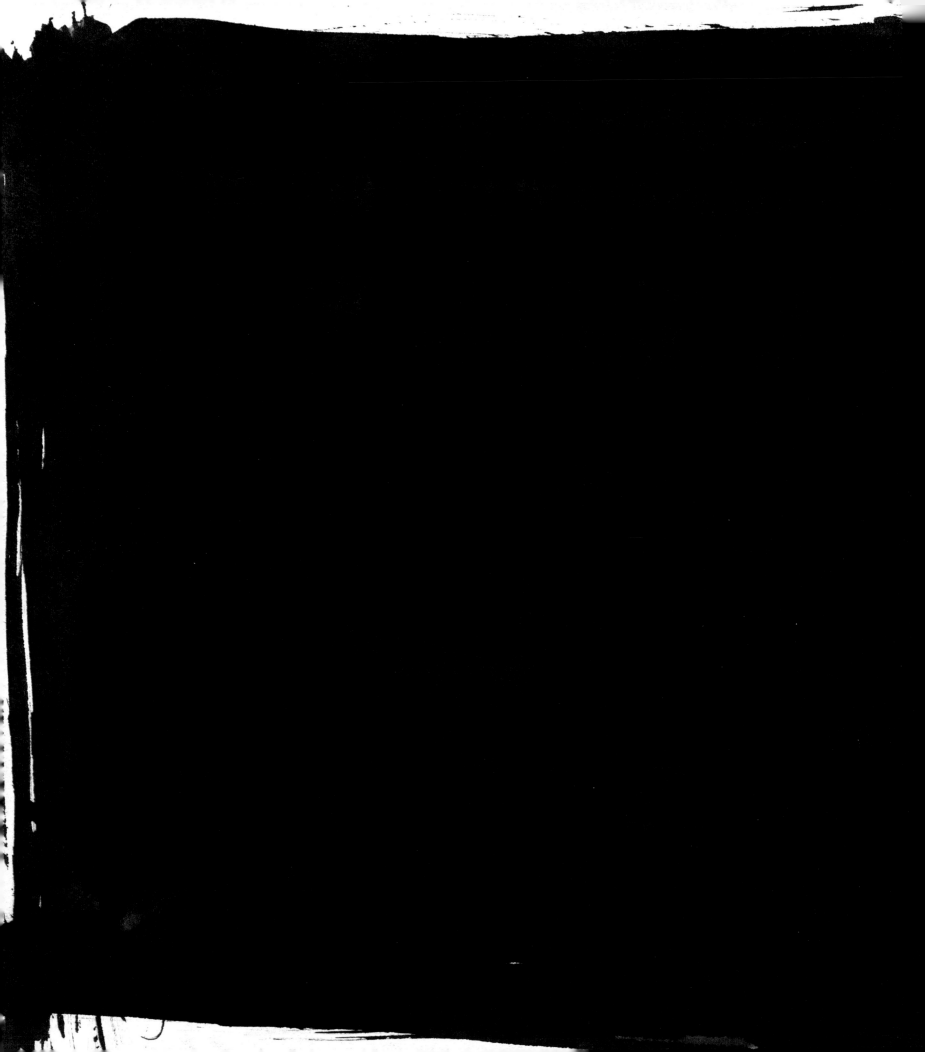

Why is there
something
instead of nothing?

What happened
before the
big bang?

does life on Earth
have any meaning?

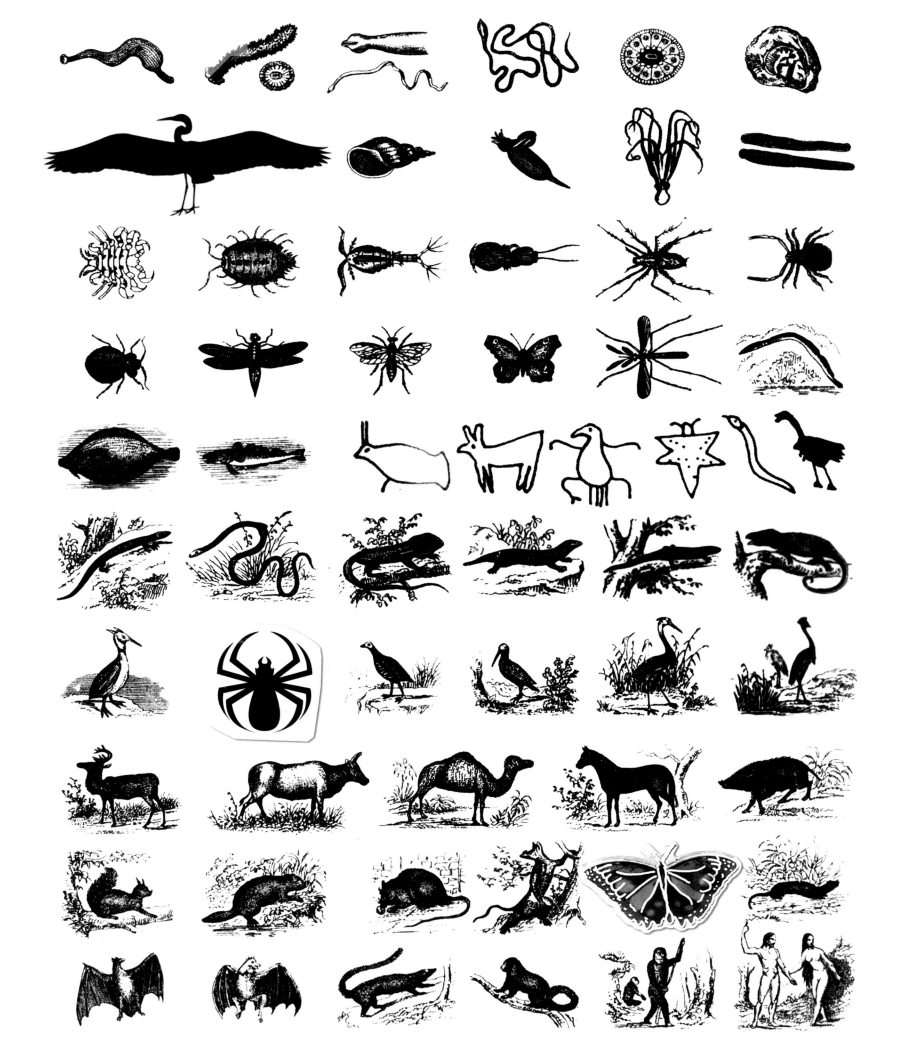

MO-JO

Pure White Chewing Gum

1¢   1¢

THE CHICLE PRODUCTS CO. NEWARK, N.J.

435. Jim Nash. *Mobilgas.* Trademark, 1933

Artone

BLIMP

MYOPIC

Filmsense

BUFFALO

We are bored in the city.
There is no longer any
temple of the sun.

the biggest problem facing us is the problem of maintaining the chain of generations. It's a problem of coherence, of meaning, of divine signal versus amateurish noise.

There is no difference
between humans
and other animals.

full blood

> I'm going to put on my voice-mail,
> soothe my aching carpal tunnel
> syndrome with 800 milligrams of
> morphine, smoke a Marlboro Light.
> Go home alone to re-runs of "Love
> Connection," my vegan microwave
> dinner, Alanis Morisette and a
> closet full of worn out clothes. Turn
> off the telephone ringer and let the
> machine eat the message from my
> workaholic boyfriend with his head
> stuck in 3-D modeling, calculus,
> a PhD and some ancient pathetic
> guilt-trip from the babe across the
> country who won't let go. Maybe
> I will take a walk on the beach and
> pick up some trash. Maybe I will
> smoke a doobie, play some guitar,
> cry over my VISA bill.

Satanic

INS

COMM

HE

ERT

ERCIAL

RE

CHAPTER 1

FORM IS POWER...

c. 1967
Designer unknown
Black Panther Party
Logo

...A WAY OF ORGA

all the
world's
a text

NIZING REALITY

... *reality organizer*

I know how to slip moods, nuances, values and perspectives right into your brain without you ever knowing it . . .

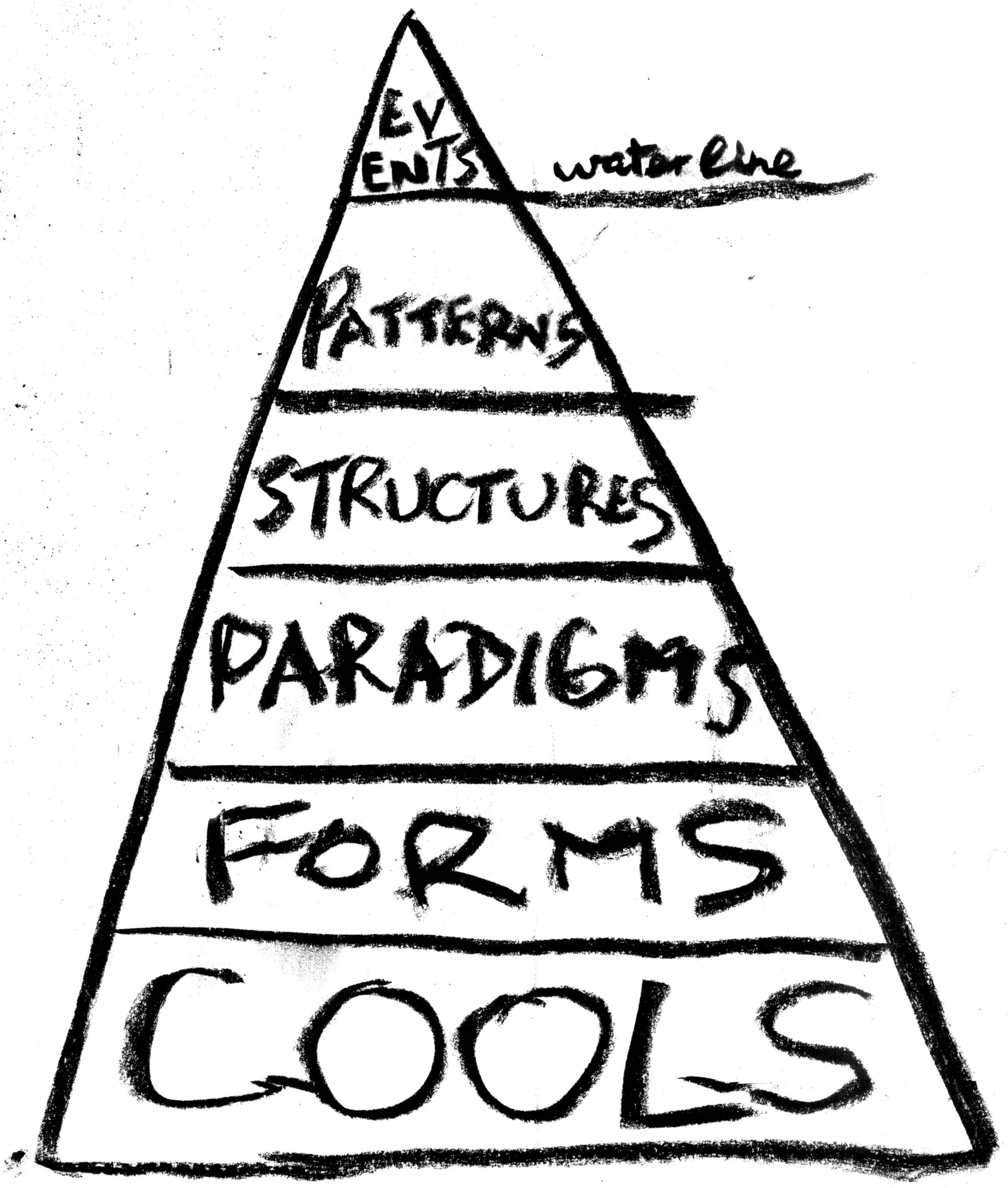

EVENTS

water line

PATTERNS

STRUCTURES

PARADIGMS

FORMS

COOLS

♪ once there was a way to get back homeward

Never go to art school. Never go to New York. Never rent a loft. Dump your font folder. Forget symmetry and colour coordination. Stop taking text from editorial that you don't read and packaging it in eye-catching ways. Walk away from your computer. Then take off. Go to India, rural China, Rio, Caracas, Belize. Mingle with the filthy rich and the dirt poor. Dig up all of the roots of terror. Make hunger, disease, cruelty, lust, greed, self-preservation and genocide your roommates. Then, when you run out of money and can't take it anymore, fly back home. Look in the mirror. Face your fears, your weaknesses, strengths, your imminent demise. Then, when all of this begins to gel into a master narrative in front of your eyes, go get a job.

Look at the designed-to-death culture of the Netherlands where everything is so beautifully designed that ultimately it adds up to just one big blah . . .

cool fascismo

TOO MUCH FORM

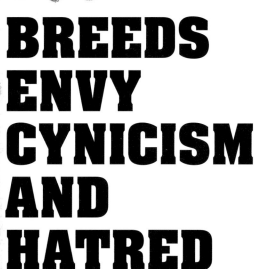

BREEDS ENVY CYNICISM AND HATRED

Or look at Japan, where an obsession with social form – too much bowing, too much rote memorization in schools, too much social ritual and hammering down of "protruding nails" – has strangled creativity and true innovation.

Our global consumer culture is the greatest example of over-design — every car, every house, every tube of lipstick, every product right down to your disposable razor is preened and pruned by teams of designers until it glistens and sparkles with cool desire.

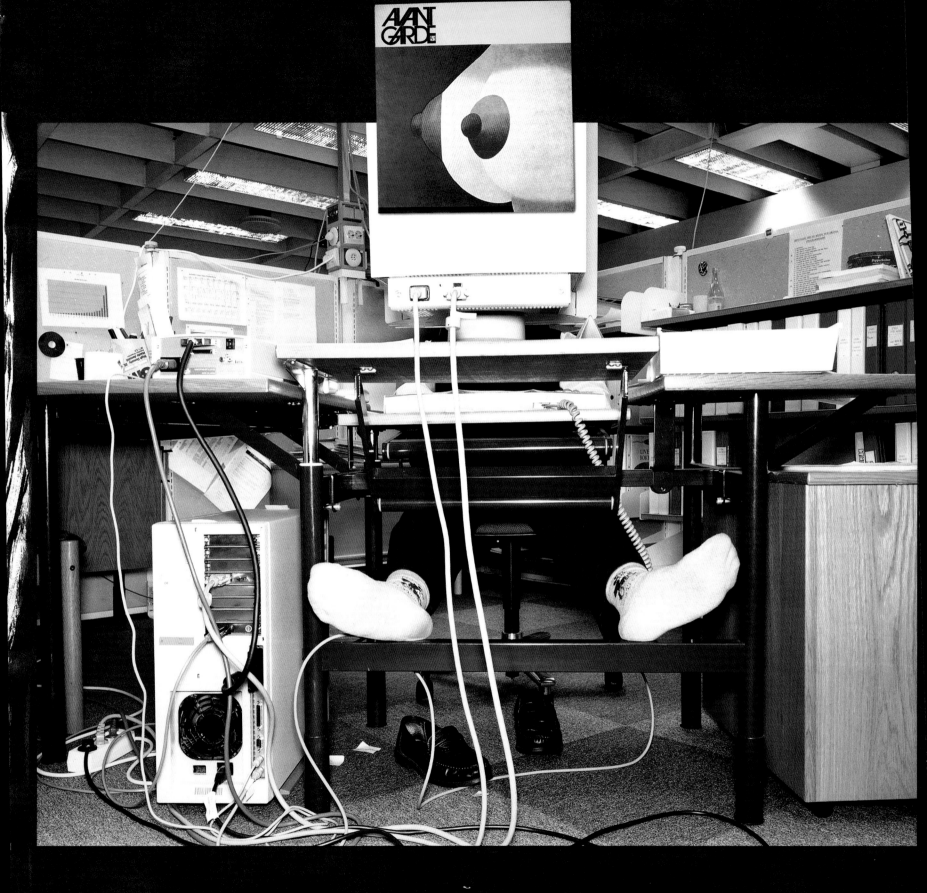

CHAPTER 2

I wanted to be an artist, but I became a graphic designer instead.

vive le fcuk!
the production of "false images" is a requirement of capitalism

Spirit in history

ЛЕН ГИЗ

КНИГИ

ПО ВСЕМ ОТРАСЛЯМ ЗНАНИЯ

ЛЕН ГИЗ

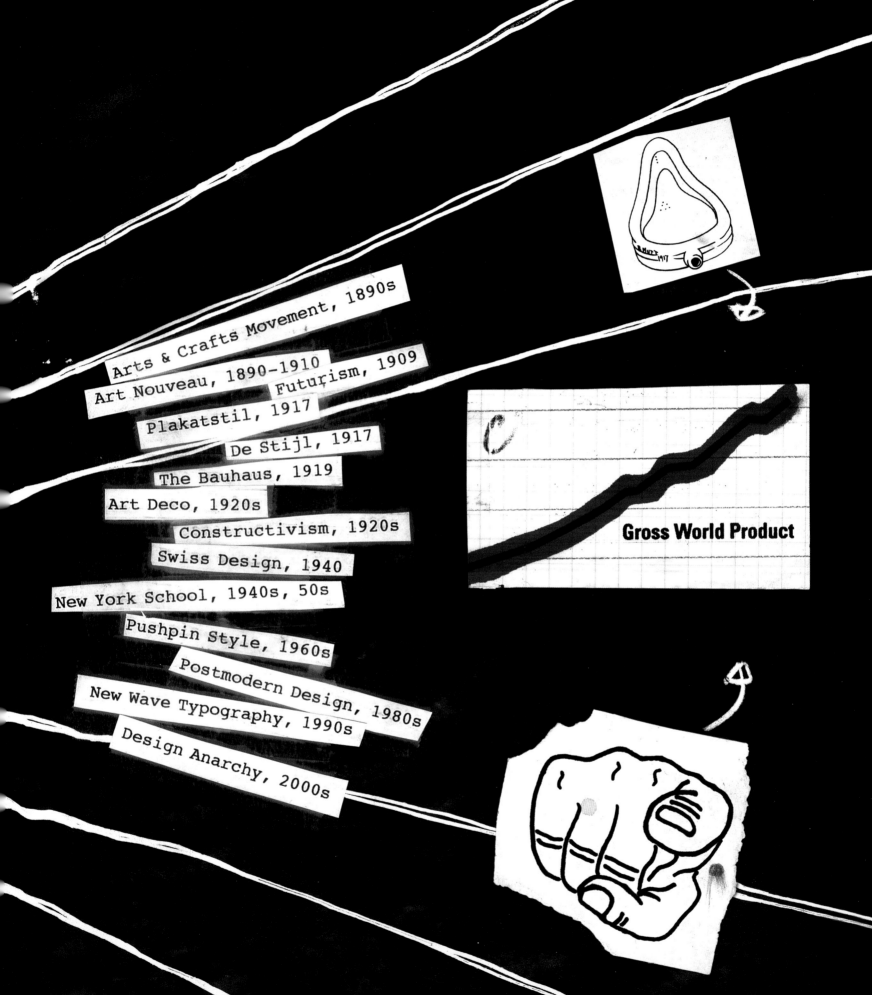

Arts & Crafts Movement, 1890s

Art Nouveau, 1890–1910

Futurism, 1909

Plakatstil, 1917

De Stijl, 1917

The Bauhaus, 1919

Art Deco, 1920s

Constructivism, 1920s

Swiss Design, 1940

New York School, 1940s, 50s

Pushpin Style, 1960s

Postmodern Design, 1980s

New Wave Typography, 1990s

Design Anarchy, 2000s

Gross World Product

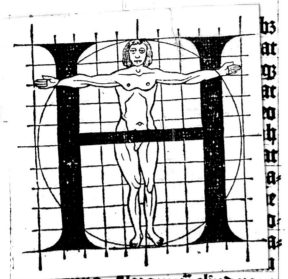

in lottanna . Nec quicqǔ aliud noue-
rat:nisi pane quo vescebat. Erat aut
ioseph pulcra facie: et decorus aspectu.
Post multos itaq dies · iniecit dña
oculos suos in ioseph : et ait. Dormi
mecǔ . Qui nequaqǔ acquiescens operi
nephario: dixit ad eā. Ecce dñs meus
omnibus michi traditis: ignorat qd
habeat in domo sua : nec quicqǔ e qd
non sit in mea potestate · vel nõ tradi-
derit michi : preter te que vxor eius es.
Quõ ergo possǔ hoc malǔ facere: z pec-
care i dñm meu? Huiuscemodi vbis p
singulos dies loquebat: et mulier mo-
lesta erat adolescenti: et ille recusabat
stuprǔ. Accidit aute quadā die ut in-
traret ioseph domǔ: et operis quippiā
absq arbitris faceret: z illa apphensa
lacinia vestimenti eius diceret. Dormi
mecǔ. Qui relicto i manu eius pallio
fugit: z egressus e foras. Cǔq vidisset
mlier vestem in manibus suis · z se esse
contemptā: vocauit ad se hoies dom9
sue: et ait ad eos . En introduxit virǔ
hebreǔ: ut illuderet nobis . Ingressus
est ad me: ut coiret mecǔ. Cǔq ego
succlamassem: z audisset vocem meā:
reliquit pallñ qd tenebam: z fugit foras. In argumentǔ ergo fidei · retentǔ
pallñ ostendit marito reuertenti domǔ·

et ait. Ingressus e ad me kuus hebre9 ·
que adduxisti: ut illuderet michi. Cǔq
audisset me clamare: reliquit pallñ
qd tenebam: z fugit foras. His audi-
tis dñs · et nimiu credulus verbis con-
iugis · iratus est valde : tradiditq ioseph in carcerem vbi vincti regis custo-
diebant: z erat ibi clausus. Fuit aute
dñs cu ioseph et misertus est illi9: z de-
dit ei gratiā in conspectu principis car-
ceris. Qui tradidit in manu illi9 vni-
uersos vinctos qui i custodia tenebāt:
et quidquid fiebat · sub ipo erat: nec no-
uerat aliquid · cūctis ei creditis . Dñs
eni erat cu illo: z oīa opera ei9 dirigebat.
His itaq gestis: accidit ut cp xl
peccaret duo eunuchi · pincerna
regis egipti et pistor · dño suo. Iratusq
q contra eos pharao · nam alter pin-
cernis preerat · alter pistoribz: misit eos
in carcerem principis militǔ · in quo
erat vinctus z ioseph. At custos carce-
ris tradidit eos ioseph: q et ministra-
bat eis. Aliquantulǔ tpis fluxerat: et illi
in custodia tenebant. Viderūtq ambo
somniǔ nocte vna: iuxta interptatio-
nem congruā sibi . Ad quos cu intro-
isset ioseph mane · z vidisset eos tristes:
sciscitatus9 e dicens. Cur tristior e hodie
solito facies vestra? Qui responderūt.
Somniǔ vidim9: et non est qui intre-
pretur nobis . Dixitq ad eos ioseph.
Nūquid nõ dei e interptatio? Referte
michi quid videritis. Narrauit prior
prepositus pincernarǔ somniǔ suǔ. Vi-
debam coram me vitem in qua erant
tres propagines crescere paulatim i gem-
mas: z post flores vuas maturescere:
calicemq pharaonis in manu mea.
Tuli ergo vuas z expressi i calicem que
tenebam: z tradidi poculǔ pharaoni.
Respondit ioseph. Hec est mpretatio

'Leshii' (Woodgoblin) No.2, 1906.

Things fall apart; the centre cannot hold

123

ABCDEFGHIJKLMN

Good morning! Have you used Pears' Soap?

the start of mind fuck

The Beethoven.—Ebonized Case.

Special Limited Price *of this Organ with bench, book & music.* **Only $75.00**

Dense with type, crowded with facts.

The New 88 Note

ANGELUS PLAYER-PIANO

If you have ever spent the evening in the company of some well-skilled, versatile pianist you have experienced in part only the numberless delights which every evening await the owner of an *Angelus* Player-Piano. Many music lovers on first hearing the *Angelus* Player-Piano have expressed their absolute amazement that the music which it enables the player to produce is so much more artistic, so superior in every way to that which any other player-piano makes possible. This for one reason is because the *Angelus* Player-Piano only is equipped with

THE MELODANT

that wonderful device which picks out and emphasizes the melody notes in such splendid contrast to those of the accompaniment. Using the *Melodant* rolls the *Angelus* player is enabled to bring out all the delicate beauties of the melody which, with the ordinary player-piano are usually lost in the maze of ornamentation which surrounds it. The *Melodant*, like the *Phrasing Lever*, the *Diaphragm Pneumatics* and the *Artistyle Music Rolls*, is a patented exclusive feature of the *Angelus*.

Refinement, culture and a happy family.

of desires

STEINWAY
The Instrument of the Immortals

There has been but one supreme piano in the history of music. In the days of Liszt and Wagner, of Rubinstein and Berlioz, the pre-eminence of the Steinway was as unquestioned as it is today. It stood then, as it stands now, the chosen instrument of the masters—the inevitable preference wherever great music is understood and esteemed.

Striking the emotional chord.

The Steinway ad on the right is already modern. It strikes an emotional chord and coins an unforgettable slogan.

LEVIATHAN

progress

« A mort! A mort! »
Voici un pays libre et fort.. C'est le pays du bon Roosevelt...
Et suspendu à une potence, les yeux fous, tirant la langue, un nègre achève de mourir. Les blancs
l'accablent de coups et d'injures. Une vieille le couvre de crachats. Une petite fille fraîche et jolie lui taille
la chair à coups de ciseaux.
Et le nègre, coupable d'avoir volé du pain, murmure dans un hoquet :
— « Oui, c'est moi le sauvage ».

the first ads were
just notices — simple
notes on posts and walls
very much like LOST DOG
notes in laundromats today—

1877

1946

1970

--- then — —
---- then --- emotion
---- then ways to improve your
                    sex life---

Joy of Living

57

3D
AND
5D

HEINZ
OVEN
BAKED
BEANS
WITH PORK AND
TOMATO SAUCE
H.J. HEINZ CO. LTD.
MADE IN ENGLAND

HEINZ BAKED BEANS

Nymphic

Look at that JOY OF LIVING ad – no ulterior motives here except to get you eating beans, or oats or shaving with a double-edged razor. Many of the early ads were truly uplifting. Then, bit by bit, a strange new element crept into advertising: a casual invitation to start comparing yourself to others. It was the birth of a kind of emotional blackmail that preyed on the tenderest spots in our self-esteem. Here the advertisers had stumbled onto one of the most psychologically powerful forms of marketing leverage ever invented, which has led to whole societies – every last one of us – looking enviously over our shoulders at each other.

1946

Yes

Coca-Cola

As a child living in an Australian immigration camp, indulgences were few and far
between. I did, however, manage to establish one private and totally extravagant
ritual: a weekly bottle of ice-cold Coca-Cola. Purchased with my allowance, and
always with a straw, which I would jiggle up and down to excite all of the bubbles.

When I left the camp, I discovered something that I had never imagined:
a competitor for the cola crown. Something called – stupidly, I thought – *Pepsi*.
It was *not* Coca-Cola. I hated it. Pepsi was the ultimate betrayal.

AMERICA NEEDS

EISENHOWER

the first presidential candidate to hire an ad agency

Down the long lane of the history yet to be written America knows that this world of ours, ever growing smaller, must avoid becoming a community of dreadful fear and hate, and be, instead, a proud confederation of mutual trust and respect.

Such a confederation must be one of equals. The weakest must come to the conference table with the same confidence as do we, protected as we are by our moral, economic, and military strength. That table, though scarred by many past frustrations, cannot be abandoned for the certain agony of the battlefield.

A B C D E F G H I J K L M

1896

1920

1950

1955

1965

1968

NOPQRSRSTUO‌‌‌XYZ

1977

1984

1988

1972

1980

1986

1996

tion

ТОВАРИЩИ
ADIEU!

I suspect that many of the
great cultural shifts that
prepare the way for political
change are largely aesthetic.

— Ballard

SHATTER

Design is one of the critical sites of struggle over the production of meaning...

Remedy

CRAcKhouse

WoolyBully

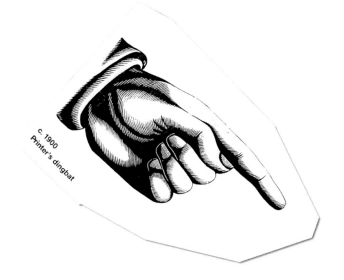

c. 1900
Printer's dingbat

I am the form of culture

I am the colourist for culture

I am the wordsmith of culture

I am the typesetter of thought

I am the editor of image

I am the court jester for the king

Cool type

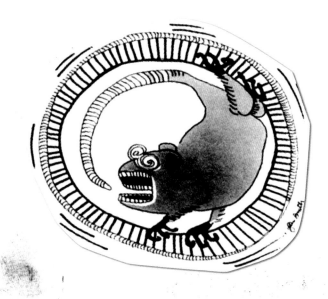

My designer day:

Sleep	7 hrs.
Eat	1.0+
	.9
Work	1.5
Doing	.2
TV	.05
Love	
the rest of my life	☺

I am a permeable membrane through which information flows...

I design tools

↓

I design dwellings

↓

I design weapons..

↓

I design cities..

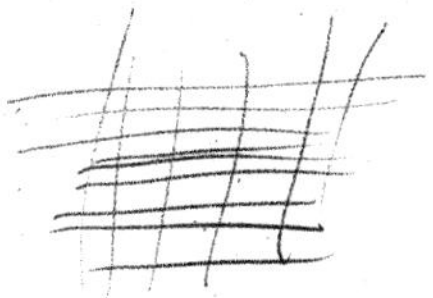

↓

I design clones..♀♀♀

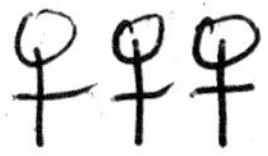

I design genes..

I design the future ...   we are here

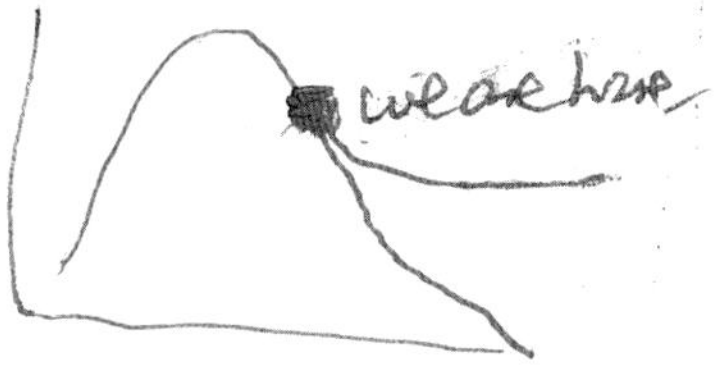

I design my own life ...

[BEMBO (c. 1929)

A profession is a rigid segment, but what goes on underneath?

I am a very powerful person

I am to the info age | what engineers were
to the age of steam
What scientists | were to the age of reason

– I set the mood | of the mental environment
– The look and lure of magazines
– The tone and pull of tv
– The give- and-take of the net

I create the envy and desire that fuels the global economy
And the cynicism that underlies our postmodern condition

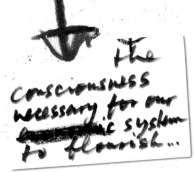

the consciousness necessary for our economic system to flourish...

It's the sheer meaninglessness of the veneers and facades that gives them such immediate impact.

I did a rough calculation once:
— about ten thousand images
  flood into my brain every day
— but only about 1% of them
  are honest and genuine
— 99% are corporate/commercial

I did a rough calculation once:
— there are about one hundred
  thousand graphic designers
  in the world
— but not even one in a hundred
  of them do any real work
— 99% are commercial hacks

After the crash, this flow will be reversed.

The Grid: a filter through which to glimpse an ideal, rationalized world

your brain clicks into a reductive mode; decisions become rote, mechanical

gains in accuracy and predictability are made at the expense of ambiguity and intuition

it's a kind of devil's bargain for logic freaks, a way to replace insight and spontaneity with a series of yes/no clicks

After the grid, inevitably, inexorably, comes the cultivation of a whole host of bad habits like neatness and balance and colour coordination

and then, POW! halfway through your life you suddenly realize that you've lost "the eye"

your instincts have been blunted, they don't come from the gut anymore

your spontaneity lies buried somewhere under a mountain of technical crap

and worse, much much worse: your empathy and ability to feel and laugh and love and cry have also eroded

you're a machine now: a cyborg.

and all because long long ago, you made that stupid decision to divvy your world up into little squares and rectangles instead of seeing it as a whole

CHAPTER 2a

Isn't this
what design is all about...?

Graphic design is the most ubiquitous of all the arts. It responds to needs at once personal and public, embraces concerns both economic and ergonomic, and is informed by many disciplines including art and architecture, philosophy and ethics, literature and language, science and politics and performance. Graphic design is everywhere, touching everything we do, everything we see, everything we buy: we see it on billboards and in ...

...making

filthy oil companies look "clean"...?

■ ■ ■ Bibles, on taxi receipts and on web sites, on birth certificates and on gift certificates, on the folded instructions inside jars of aspirin and on the thick pages of children's picture books. Graphic design is the boldly directional arrows on street signs and the blurred, frenetic typography on the title sequence to E.R. It is the bright green logo for the New York Jets and the ■ ■ ■

...making

spaghetti sauce look like it's been cooked by grandma...?

■ ■ ■ monochromatic front page of The Wall Street Journal. It is hang tags in clothing stores, postage stamps and food packaging, fascist propaganda posters and brainless junk mail. Graphic design is complex combinations of words and pictures, numbers and charts, photographs and illustrations that, in order to succeed, demand the clear thinking of a particularly thoughtful individual ■ ■ ■

WARNING!
Genetically
KRAFTED
Foods

...making
junky condos look hip?

■ ■ ■ who can orchestrate these elements so that they all add up to something distinctive, or useful, or playful, or surprising, or subversive, or somehow memorable. Graphic design is a popular art and a practical art, an applied art and an ancient art. Simply put, it is the art of visualizing ideas.
— JESSICA HELFAND

Mondran
Luxury Condos

Welcome to a life worth living

How we see design

We believe that innovative solutions with strategic business advantages occur at the intersection of business, technology and user needs, as the red circle indicates. This diagram locates some of our recent projects within this model.

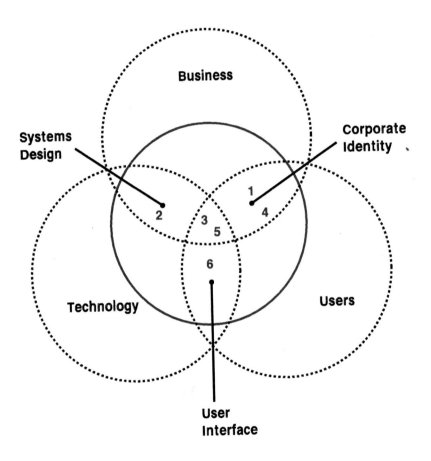

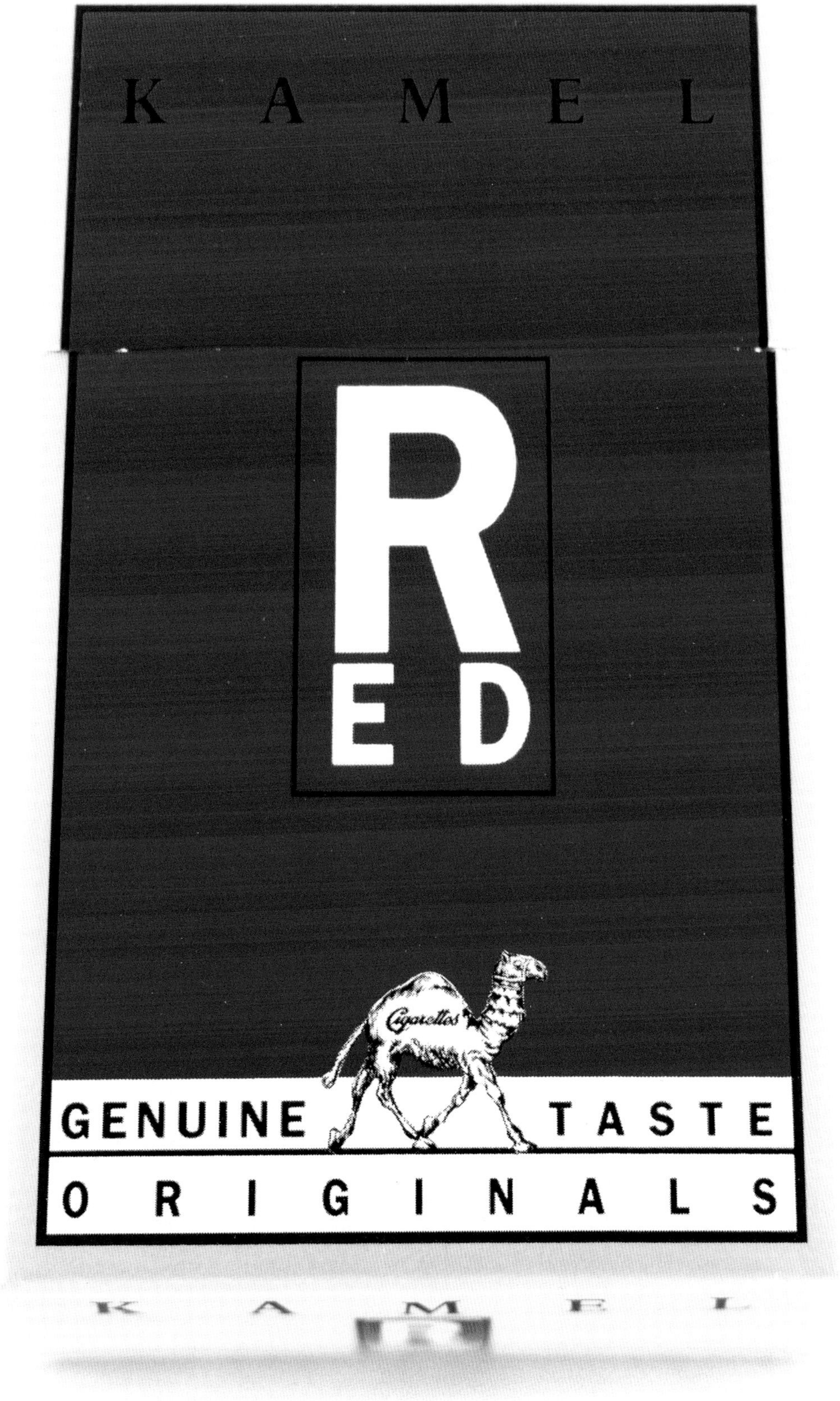
KAMEL
RED
Cigarettes
GENUINE TASTE
ORIGINALS
KAMEL

It's about the struggle between individuals with jagged passion in their work and today's faceless corporate committees, which claim to understand the needs of the mass audience, and are removing the idiosyncrasies, polishing the jags, creating a thought-free, passion-free, cultural mush that will not be hated nor loved by anyone. By now, virtually all media, architecture, product and graphic design have been freed from ideas, individual passion, and have been relegated to a role of corporate servitude, carrying out corporate strategies and increasing stock prices. Creative people are now working for the bottom line.

Tibor Kalman
New York, June 1998

catch the eye.

I'M A PROFESSIONAL. I SERVE "COMMUNICATIONS NEEDS" OF MY CLIENTS . . . I DELIVER "DESIGN SOLUTIONS." OVER THE YEARS

stimulate desire.

I'VE LEARNED, LIKE A WELL SEASONED PROSTITUTE, TO PUT MY PERSONAL FEELINGS ASIDE AND "MAINTAIN A COOL OBJECTIVITY

move product.

ABOUT THE MOST INTIMATE OF HUMAN ACTIVITIES, DISCIPLINING MY PERSONAL RESPONSES TO DELIVER AN IMPARTIAL AND CONSIS-

win awards.

TENT PRODUCT TO MY CLIENTS."

the
capitalist
imagination

You can keep knocking about in the pomo hall of mirrors, layering on the polish and creating warm nuclear glows around your clients' brands. You can spend the rest of your creative life massaging egos and collecting gaudy awards. Or – and here's the great moment of truth – you can opt out, you can come over to the other side and join the search for a new kind of meaning.

Don't work for
companies that
want you to die
for them
Tibor

You are in demand
IF YOU CAN DRAW!

Make Money with your brush and pen! If you like to draw, sketch, or paint, take the Free Talent Test. No fee. No obligation. Mail this coupon TODAY!

ART INSTRUCTION, INC., Dept. 4961
500 S. 4th Street, Minneapolis 15, Minnesota
Please send me your FREE Talent Test.

Name_____Age_____
Address_____Phone_____
City_____Zone____County_____
State_____Occupation_____

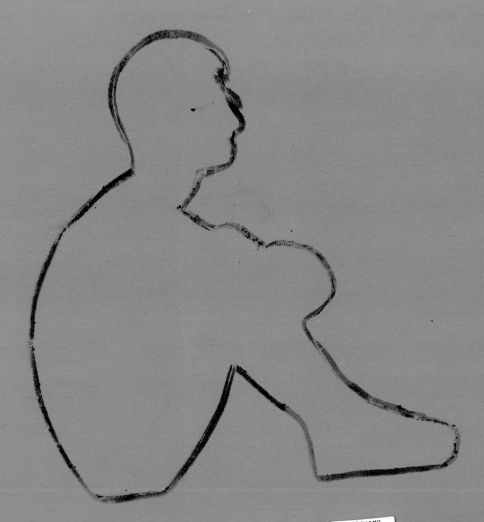

elements of style. Apollo is the god of form, clarity, solid contours, bright dreams, and, above all, individuality. Sculpture, architecture, the Homeric world of the gods, the epic spirit—all of these are Apollonian. Dionysus, by contrast, is the wild god of transport, rapture, ecstasy, "the orgiastic." Music and dance are the preferred forms. The appeal of the Apollonian lies in the fact that the artifice is never forgotten for a single instant and the awareness of distances is retained. In the Dionysian arts, by contrast, boundaries are fluid. A person in the thrall of music, dance, or other such artistic exploit loses his distance. The "Dionysian reveler" does not see himself from without, whereas the Apollonian remains reflexive; he enjoys his enthusiasm without succumbing to it. The

CHAPTER 3

Are you a: ○   cool maker
             ○   cool breaker

COMMERCIAL MAGAZINES ARE POISONED MINDSPACE

Experiences That Drive Magazine Use

Brand Experiences

Consumer Connection Sweetspot

Brand Communications
• Creative
• Placements
• Marketing Programs

— THE ADS RULE

— THERE IS NO WAY AROUND THEM

— THEY FRAGMENT THE SPACE

ADBUSTERS

Magazine

ADBUSTERS SPRING 2000   VOL.8 NO.1

220 g $5.75

US/CAN $5.75 UK £3.95 ¥1200

Wilderness is everywhere: worms in the compost, lichens on the balcony, people living off the grid.

We were a bunch of burnt-out activists tired of environmentalism, feminism and all of the other -isms. We felt that all these movements had peaked long ago, that they had become stagnant and now belonged to history. And we were disillusioned with the political left as a whole – quite a brave notion in the early 1990s, when anyone who dared to badmouth the left was immediately expelled from the fold.

We yearned for something new. *Culture* kept popping up in our brainstorms. Culture was exciting. Who creates it? Who controls it? We had this nasty feeling that "we the people" were slowly but surely losing our power to sing the songs and tell the stories and generate our culture from the bottom up. More and more, the stories were being fed to us top-down by TV networks, ad agencies and corporations "with something to sell as well as to tell." This idea that we may be witnessing a cultural coup d'état mesmerized us. Had we stumbled onto the next great social activist movement? After the civil rights movement, after women's liberation, and after the environmental movement, perhaps the next great social movement would be *culture jamming* – taking the storytelling, culture-generating power back from commercial and corporate forces.

We were a visually driven bunch. I was an experimental and documentary filmmaker, Bill Schmalz was a wilderness cinematographer, and many others were photographers, illustrators, designers. We were all sick of that old lefty magazine mold (still alive and kicking today) in which page after page of heavy texttexttexttext is taken for granted, and you thank your lucky stars if a cartoon is thrown in every now and again. We dreamt of a new kind of lefty rag – a slick-subversive mindbomb full of intimate epiphanies, geopolitical insights and *ad hominem* attacks; a magazine that would fire up the political activist scene with graphic punch and unflinching works of art.

We had no intention of running ads (with a name like *Adbusters* who would want to buy our space anyway?) but all of the advisors and consultants we talked to warned us not to go that route. I remember one crusty old industry pro getting all worked up over a bottle of Aussie red shouting, "Go ahead, you fucking idiot . . . but I warn you, within a year you'll be a burned out wreck, you'll have a garage full of unsold magazines . . . everyone will start deserting you like rats jumping off a sinking ship. Eventually you won't be able to make your mortgage payments, your wife will divorce you and you'll regret this stupidity for the rest of your life."

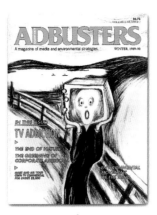

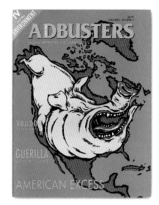

The flow in the first few issues of *Adbusters* was achieved by laying all the spreads and articles side by side over a half-dozen picnic tables. We would walk around the room, moving pages and spreads and bits of paper around the tables until, as the deadline neared, you could walk from the first table to the last without feeling any emotional bumps or conceptual discontinuities.

A year later we moved to a smaller basement and started using a three-hole binder full of plastic sleeves. Instead of moving pages around picnic tables, we juggled sleeves around the mockup. This turned out to be one of our finest innovations. Photographs, blocks of text and any scraps of scribbled-on paper could be easily slipped in and out of the sleeves, while comments could be hand-written right on the plastic with a grease pencil. Many people could contribute simultaneously to the creative flow, slipping in their suggestions and brain waves while checking out what the others had done. Flipping though the mockup you could feel – physically feel – the reader's final experience of negotiating your magazine, a visceral sense of the final product.

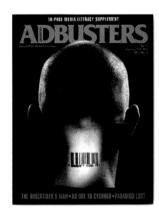

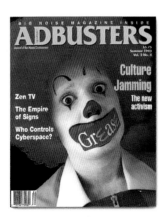

#14

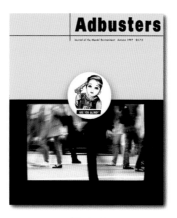

#19

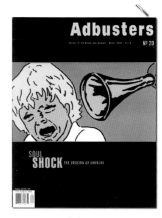

#20

#27

For the first seven or eight years we didn't shine. Despite all of our anger, guts and passion, *Adbusters* looked pretty drab. An occasional spoof ad would cause a shiver of excitement. An occasional piece of writing would hit the mark. Yet we were half of a million dollars in the red.

A breakthrough came when Chris Dixon joined as art director. He taught us a few tricks and what a certain level of *feinschmeck* could do.

In 1998 Chris and I visited Tibor Kalman in New York. We showed him the *First Things First Manifesto* that we had reprinted. He said we should do it again. *First Things First 2000*, in our Autumn 1999 issue (#27), managed to prick the conscience of designers all over the world.

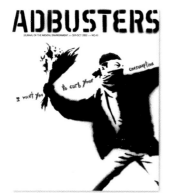

#43

#49

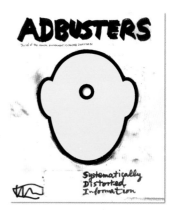

#51

ADBUSTERS

No. 37

SPECIAL DOUBLE ISSUE.

DESIGN ANARCHY

DESIGN ANARCHY

SEPTEMBER/OCTOBER 2001 · VOL. 9 NO. 5

US/CAN $7.95 UK £4.50 ¥1500

VOL. 9 NO. 5 SEPT/OCT 2001

Another leap forward happened in 2001 when Jonathan Barnbrook guest art-directed the *Design Anarchy* issue (#37). After that some of the most preeminent artists in the world like Cindy Sherman, Jeff Wall, Damien Hirst, Jeff Koons, James Victore, Andre Serrano, and Pipilotti Rist started contributing their work, often free of charge.

62

#56

It was not until the Battle of Seattle that our magazine really started taking off. Our circulation soared to 120,000. Suddenly we had money to burn and we burned it good. I thought, "My god, we've finally done it – we've finally got ourselves a slick-subversive rag."

Then s.11 happened. Perversely, that became our high point. We grabbed stuff from all over the charged-up mindscape and, for the first time, an issue gelled from cover to cover in a seamless gestalt.

ADBUSTERS

JOURNAL OF THE MENTAL ENVIRONMENT >> JAN/FEB 2002 >> NO 39

how to create a non-commercial magazine aesthetic (and survive without ad revenue)

FIRST YOU KILL THE PAGE NUMBERS
because they just disrupt the flow

THEN YOU KILL THE TABLE OF CONTENTS
because it's the signature of commercial compartmentalization

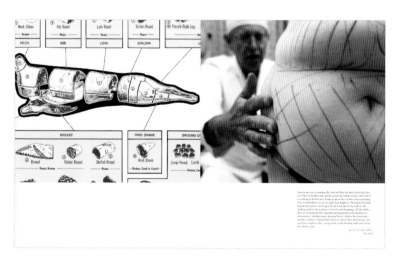

THEN YOU KILL THE DECKS & HEADS
because, in a seamless flow, there are no beginnings

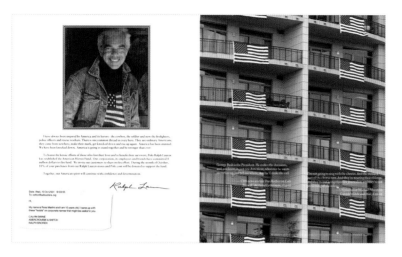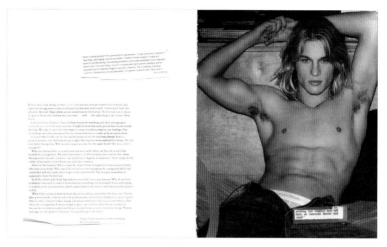

THEN YOU TAKE SOME OF THE LETTERS TO THE EDITOR AND SPRINKLE THEM THROUGHOUT
(a very democratic move)

> " There is something deeply suffocating about life today in the prosperous west. Bourgeoisification, the suburbanisation of the soul, proceeds at an unnerving pace. Tyranny becomes docile and subservient, and soft totalitarianism prevails, as obsequious as a wine waiter. Nothing is allowed to distress and unsettle us. The politics of the playgroup rules us all.
>
> — *J.G. Ballard* "

YEAR'S END, ALL CORNERS OF THIS FLOATING WORLD, SWEPT
— *BASHO*

YOU COLLECT INSPIRING QUOTES AND BITS OF TEXT FROM ALL OVER AND PLACE THEM
INTO YOUR MOCKUP LIKE PIECES IN A JIGSAW PUZZLE

YOU USE PAGE-SIZED PUNCTUATION TO SMOOTH OUT CONCEPTUAL DISCONTINUITIES
(as if your magazine were one long sentence)

THEN YOU TEAR OUT ADS FROM OTHER MAGAZINES AND USE THEM AS COUNTERPOINT

YOU RIP THEM UP AND USE THEM AS BACKDROP
(a neat reversal of capitalist appropriation)

AS THE DEADLINE APPROACHES, YOU START WRITING & DOODLING (pissing) ALL OVER THE MOCKUP
—> looking for ways to meld pic&text together into a stream-of-consciousness
—> getting spread after spread to magically hang together in a kind of meta-language of concept & mood
—> creating longer and longer narratives until your whole mockup gels into
one big story that reads like a comic book from cover to cover . . .

 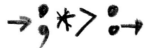  

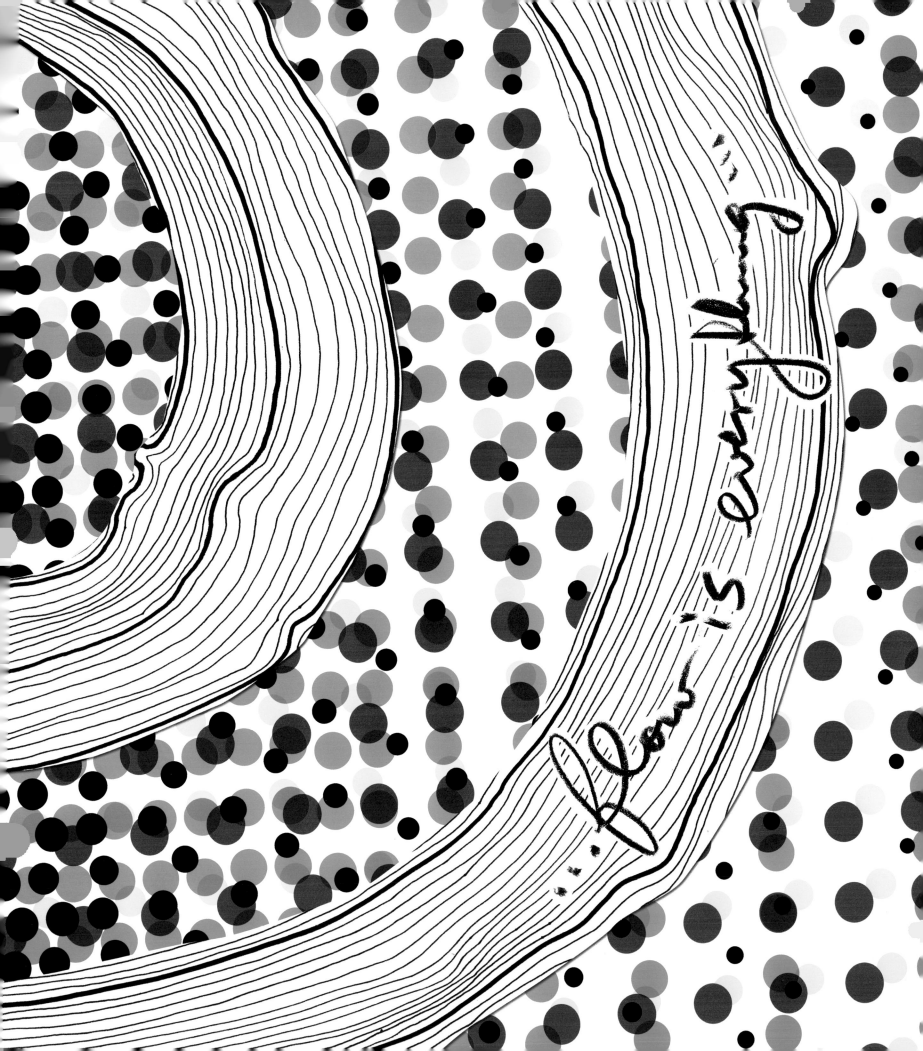

it's what makes a magazine work...
it's the highest of highs...

it's what your life is all about...

flow, flow, flow...

CHAPTER 4

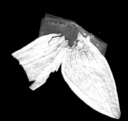

"After the crash, there will be fewer resources, fewer products, less advertising . . . and fewer designers. There will be no more sumptuous coffee table annuals, no more mass-mailings on creamy paper inviting members to attend gala events in distant cities. Phone messages will be left unanswered, e-mail unreturned, websites unsurfed. There will be less paper and more trees, fewer cars and more walking, less airtime and more air. People will feel less assaulted by images and products and more attentive to the spaces between them. And they will begin to call these undesigned spaces 'nature.'"

boreal toad endangered

the quiet tanglepond
a frog jumps in
plop!

population

temp.

Atlantic Cod

The self-organizing principles of markets that have emerged in human cultures over the past 10,000 years are in conflict with the self-organizing principles of ecosystems that have evolved over the past 3.5 billion years.

We affirm that the world's magnificence has been enriched by a new beauty: the beauty of speed. A racing car whose hood is adorned with great pipes, like serpents of explosive breath—a roaring car that seems to ride on grapeshot is more beautiful than the *Victory of Samothrace*.

Oldsmobile

12th Year

Power—Silence—Speed,—with Safety

OLDS MOTOR WORKS

The people of the future will gaze back in ghastly awe upon our time . . . a time of waste and abandon on a scale so vast it knocked the human enterprise on planet earth out of whack for a thousand years.

The world's largest iceberg has just split in two

THE HOUSE
THE CAR
THE THINGS

[ENDGAME]

The richest and most accessible mineral deposits are exhausted; old-growth forest have been cleared; oil secrets itself away deeper and deeper into the Earth's darkness. Fish stocks decline. Potable water proves itself an ever-more-costly commodity. The technology that we've relied on to make our lives more comfortable begins to degrade them.

The spread of agriculture and the industrial revolution brings plenitude and population. Nature remains abundant, but cities, freeways, airports and industrial parks bring a kind of landscape the world has never known.

For thousands of generations, we humans were a part of nature, we *were* nature.

Then came the beginning of our divergence: the digging of wells and mines, the damming and channelling of rivers, the draining of swamps. Our barely perceptible footprint grew deeper, larger, more clearly delineated – like a field instead of a meadow, a road instead of a path.

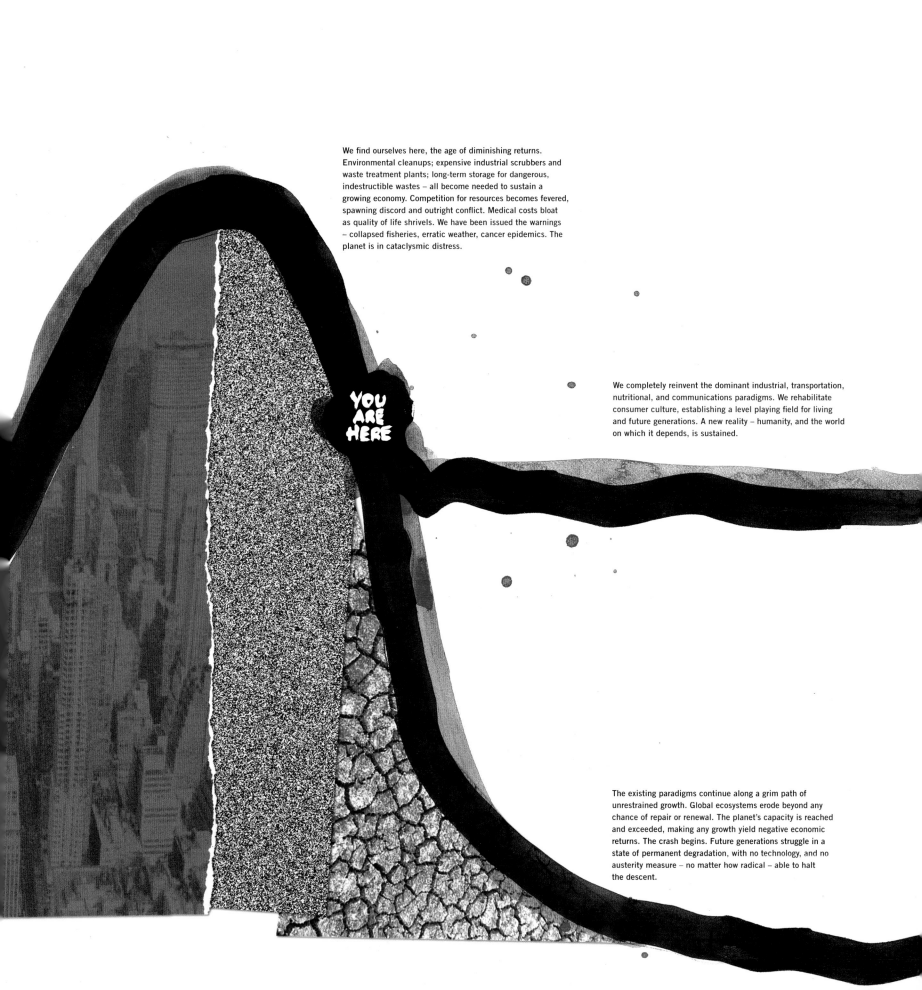

We find ourselves here, the age of diminishing returns. Environmental cleanups; expensive industrial scrubbers and waste treatment plants; long-term storage for dangerous, indestructible wastes – all become needed to sustain a growing economy. Competition for resources becomes fevered, spawning discord and outright conflict. Medical costs bloat as quality of life shrivels. We have been issued the warnings – collapsed fisheries, erratic weather, cancer epidemics. The planet is in cataclysmic distress.

YOU ARE HERE

We completely reinvent the dominant industrial, transportation, nutritional, and communications paradigms. We rehabilitate consumer culture, establishing a level playing field for living and future generations. A new reality – humanity, and the world on which it depends, is sustained.

The existing paradigms continue along a grim path of unrestrained growth. Global ecosystems erode beyond any chance of repair or renewal. The planet's capacity is reached and exceeded, making any growth yield negative economic returns. The crash begins. Future generations struggle in a state of permanent degradation, with no technology, and no austerity measure – no matter how radical – able to halt the descent.

On the day the world ends
A bee circles a clover,
A Fisherman mends a glimmering net.
Happy porpoises jump in the sea,
By the rainspout young sparrows are playing
And the snake is gold-skinned as it should always be.

On the day the world ends
Women walk through fields under their umbrellas
A drunkard grows sleepy at the edge of a lawn,
Vegetable peddlers shout in the street
And a yellow-sailed boat comes nearer the island,
The voice of a violin lasts in the air
And leads into a starry night.

And those who expected lightning and thunder
Are disappointed.
And those who expected signs and archangels' trumps
Do not believe it is happening now.
As long as the sun and the moon are above,
As long as the bumblebee visits a rose,
As long as rosy infants are born
No one believes it is happening now.

Only a white-haired old man, who would be a prophet,
Yet is not a prophet, for he's much too busy,
Repeats while he binds his tomatoes:
There will be no other end of the world,
There will be no other end of the world.

Czeslaw Milosz

EVERYBODY LOVES A GOOD SMOKE!

rial blood to an organ, the organ dies. When you cut the flow of nature into people's lives, their spirit dies. It's as simple as that.

When you cut off arte-

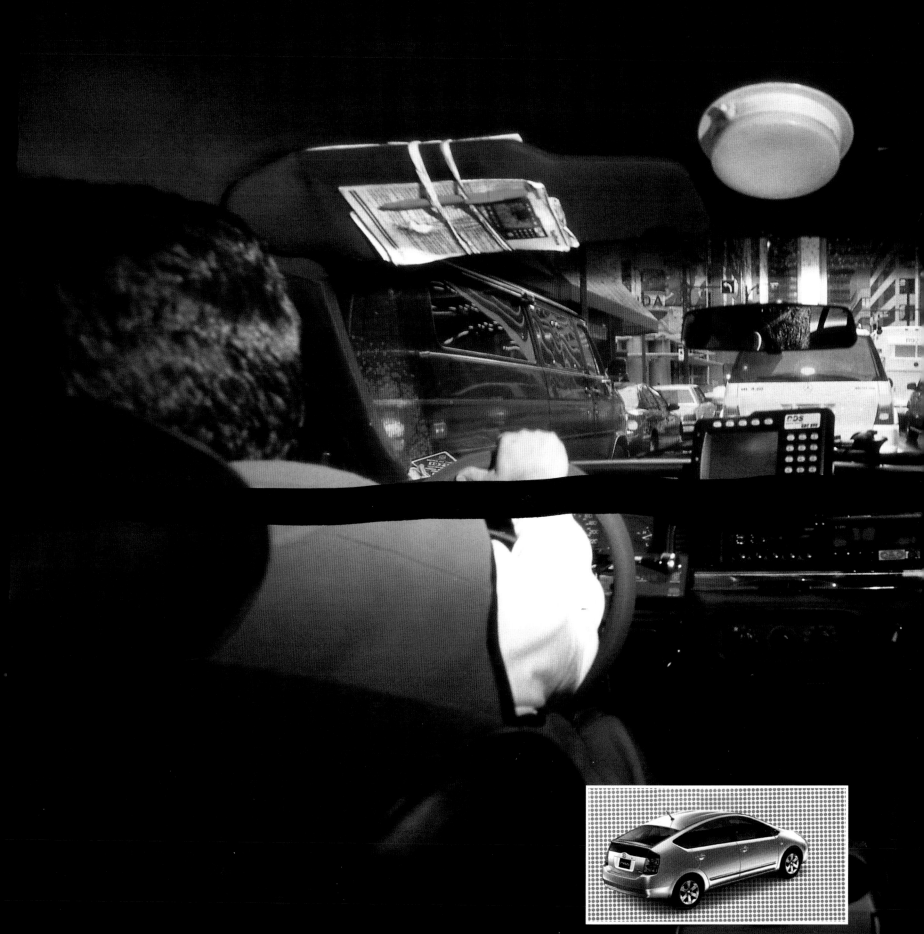

YOU ARE IN CONTROL

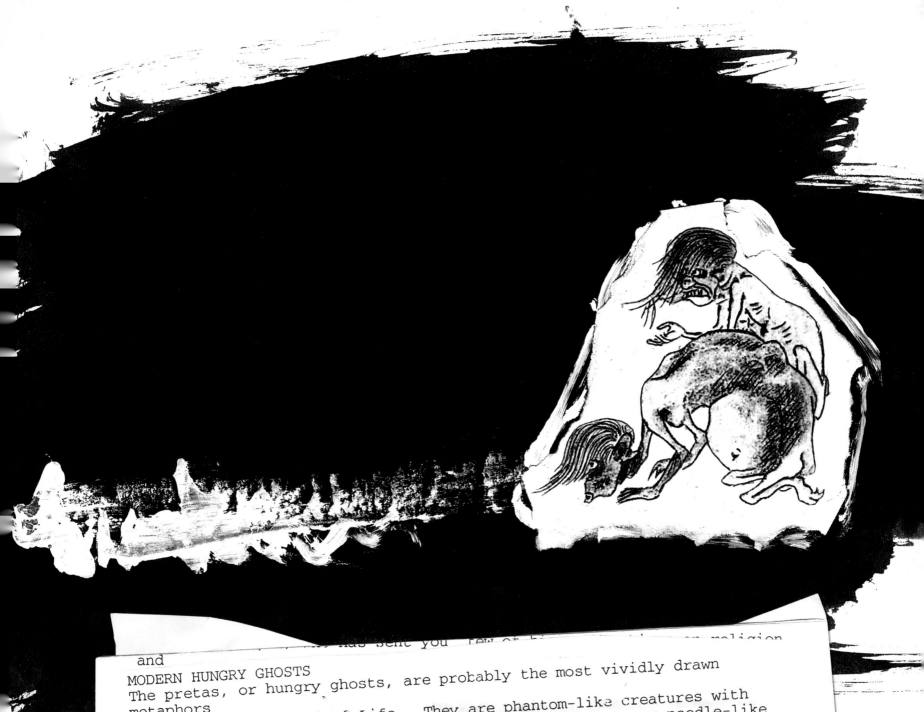

and

MODERN HUNGRY GHOSTS

The pretas, or hungry ghosts, are probably the most vividly drawn metaphors
in the Buddhist Wheel of Life. They are phantom-like creatures with
withered limbs, grossly bloated bellies, and long, narrow needle-like
necks. They demand impossible satisfactions so they have stretched
necks---hungry and demanding the impossible. They are searching for
gratification for old unfulfilled needs whose time has passed. Their
ghost
like state is representative of their attachment to the past. They live
in
past wants and desires.

life

power

INS

COMM

HE

ERT

ERCIAL

RE

WE ARE DROWNING IN A MEDIA-FED FANTASY. WE ARE THE FIRST GENERATION IN HUMAN HISTORY TO HAVE OUR LIVES SHAPED – NOT BY NATURE – BUT BY THE BEGUILING IMAGES OF THE ELECTRONIC MEDIA. WE SPEND MORE HOURS WATCHING NATURE SHOWS THAN EXPERIENCING THE REAL THING; MORE TIME LAUGHING AT TV JOKES THAN JOKING AROUND OURSELVES; MORE EVENINGS EXPERIENCING VIRTUAL SEX THAN ACTUALLY HAVING SEX OURSELVES. AS WE FOREGO THE ROLE OF PARTICIPANT IN THE REAL WORLD, WE BECOME SPECTATORS IN THE FLICKERING WORLD OF MAKE BELIEVE.

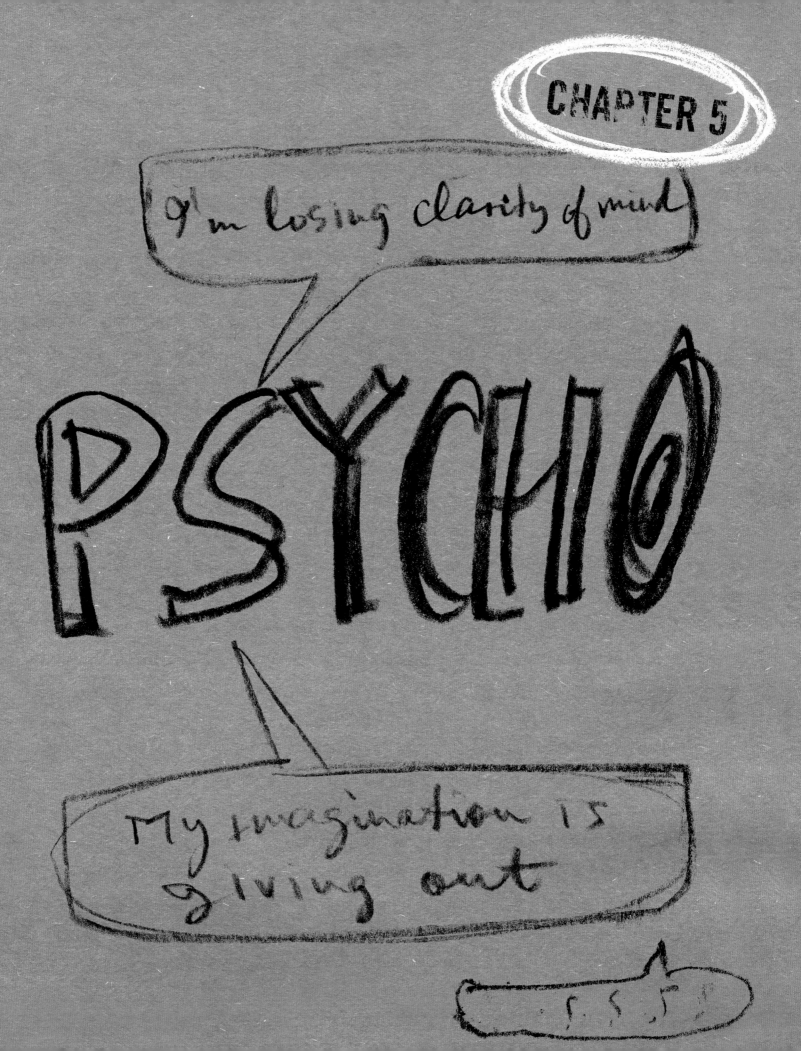

TWO SIDES OF THE SAME COIN

eco ⟷ psycho

pollution ⟷ noise

biotoxin ⟷ infotoxin

toxic environment ⟷ toxic culture

eco collapse ⟷ mental breakdown

ecocide

suicide

Don't stumble. Don't fall. Lose your mental stride and you'll end up depressed, bipolar or schizophrenic. You could wake up in a post-war mental ward feeling like your whole past is a hazy dream. And believe it, there are millions out there who know the story: gradually your motivation dims, your sleep becomes disturbed, and you lose clarity of mind. Then you're in big fucking trouble, for there's a threshold here, and once you've crossed over it's tough as hell getting back. Sometimes meds help, or even institutionalization, but more often than not you become dependent on the drugs, and then there's a second monkey on your back.

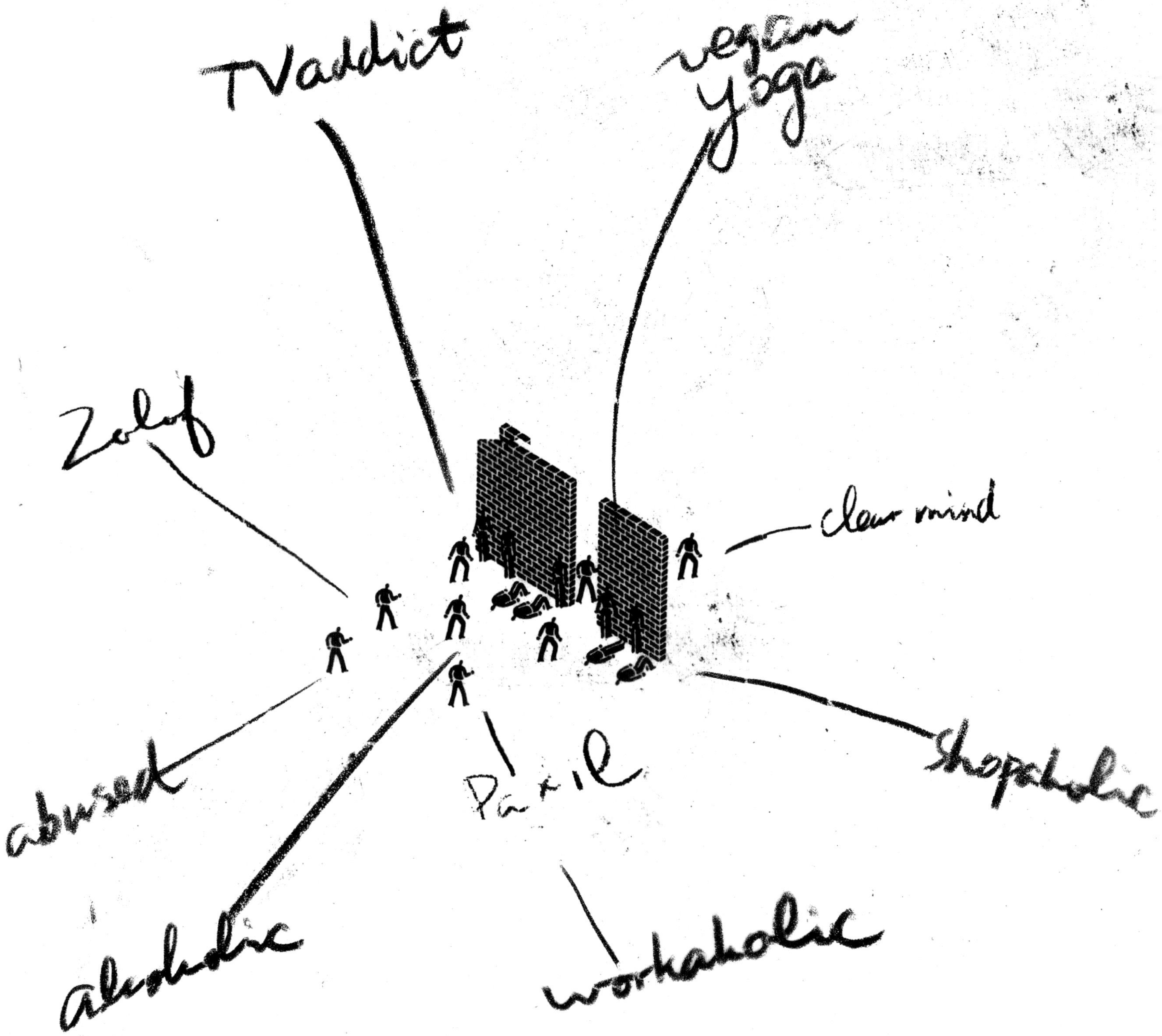

TVaddict

vegan
yoga

Zolof

clear mind

abused

shopaholic

alcoholic

Paxil

workaholic

I CAN'T GO TO WORK, I'M HAVING AN EMOTIONAL
BREAKDOWN

I CAN'T GO TO WORK,   I'M HAVING AN EMOTIONAL BREAKTHROUGH

> I strike up a conversation with a cute guy that just entered the room. He's wearing a blue and grey
> hoodie and I can't help but wonder if he's a good kisser. I giggle and introduce myself, ask him his
> name, slowly taking a sip of my rye and coke. The music is thumping and people are everywhere. He
> offers me beer, I say, "Only if it's cold." He hands me one, I smile, talk a little bit longer, then excuse
> myself. I feel sick. I already threw up once and it's going to happen again. I tell a friend to watch my
> beer and run to the bathroom. Someone happens to be in there. Bastards. I pace around the hall, holding
> my vomit down. He opens the door and I run in, throwing up instantly. Some one pounds on the door
> yelling for me to hurry up. I scream at them in between my gags. They keep pounding so I cut it short
> and rinse out my mouth. I open the door and stare them down with the evilest look I have.
>
> One of them comes up to me later. She's the blonde one with noticeable roots and badly applied eye
> shadow. Tanya was telling me earlier how much she hates her and that she tried to pick up her boyfriend
> once before. Tanya beat me up with her friend when I was 13 so I don't really say anything around her.
> The girl apologizes to me and tries to start a conversation. I roll my eyes and pay attention to that cute
> guy I met earlier. After a while I tell her to go away. She asks why. Like I really need a reason. I tell her
> she's too nice and it's making me sick. I mutter for her to go away and wave my hand in a dismissive
> flick. She almost crawls away. I tell Tanya, who giggles and hugs me.
>
> The night moves on. I mix more drinks and get incredibly drunk. Swaying my hips, making crude
> gestures, and giving seductive looks to that cute guy. I forgot his name already but I'll find out later.
> Pitch black. Nothing. Nowhere. No memory. I'm at home and it's 11:00 am. I feel odd and discover I
> only have one shoe. I sigh and phone my mother on her cell phone and ask her if we're going to go to
> my cousin's today. She says yes. I jump in the shower and get ready.
>
> All weekend, we enjoy swimming, canoeing and most of nature's luxuries. I feel at peace with myself
> and the world. The ride back is horrible. I dread coming back and fear exactly what I did at that party.
> My mother drops me off and leaves me with my ghost of a father. I talk to Laura at work and she says
> that I just disappeared from the party. I told her I went home. I'm in the clear. I tell her about my boycott
> of McDonald's, which lasted for 5 months or so until I was too poor to eat unless it was the McDeal
> Meal. I suggest that we do it again.
>
> After work I head to my empty house and lay down with my kitty. I look through a YM magazine and
> notice all the perfect people then look at the bulge at my stomach and cringe. My dad phones me and
> tells me he's going for supper and asks if I would rather eat McDonald's, Wendy's or A&W. I pause and
> think. He gets impatient. I ask for a McNugget meal. He hangs up. I feel ashamed. He drops off the food
> for me then disappears again. I nibble on my french fries, eat a few nuggets and get sick of it. I do a little
> housework and sit on the computer staring blankly at the screen. Laura and I go rent movies. We watch
> a documentary on Africa's economy called "Life and Debt." It's sad when you realize just how hard
> life is for other people. Laura leaves after we skim through the latest Adbusters. Bedtime soon. Work
> tomorrow.
>
> I wash my face, brush my teeth and apply skin-firming lotion. Staring into the mirror I hate what I see. I
> try to find some familiarity in my eyes. Nothing. I hold myself in contempt. The other day I was thinking
> of suicide but thought of how selfish it was. Then I tell myself I'm getting my nails done professionally
> tomorrow and my eyebrows waxed. It'll all be okay because I will look good. I walk into the bedroom
> and lay down thinking that I should really buy a gym pass and start working out. I imagine how good
> I will look once school starts. I'll be able to wear the short skirts and tight shirts and make the boys
> drool. Then I think why do I have to work on the external view of me just to love myself on the inside?
> I've been working on loving myself but I can't do it. I see the flaws, the ugly scars on my legs, the love
> handles and my odd shaped feet and I can't help but be disgusted. I lust after a toned body and long legs.
> I lust to be someone else.
>
> Helen Knott

Adbusters

Journal of the Mental Environment   Winter 1998 $5.75

SOUL
SHOCK THE EROSION OF EMPATHY

.Back in 1989 we dubbed *Adbusters* magazine a "journal of the mental environment," and ever since we've been busily exploring this cerebral terrain. We've watched the battle of the mind intensify as thousands of commercial messages are discharged into each of our brains every single day. We've tracked the rise of addictions, anxiety and mood disorders as they have grown into what some public health officials describe as an epidemic of despair. We've watched the media corporations merge, consolidate and vertically integrate until a handful of them now control the majority of all the news and entertainment across the planet. And throughout the journey, we've marveled at human resiliency, wondering just how toxic our mental environment would have to get before some threshold of tolerance is exceeded, before people start demanding a cleaner, less cluttered, more democratic mass media.

It hasn't happened yet. Few people are throwing their TVs out the window in hopes of hitting Rupert Murdoch. No anti-trust actions are pending against Viacom, Time Warner or News Corp. It's true that independent, community-based alternatives are breaking new ground everyday, but progress on the big issues has been slow and victories scarce. In the eyes of the general public, the media reform movement hasn't quite gelled. The reality is this: we need a total revolution in how we relate to the media, and only a groundswell of public support is going to get us there.

Remember what launched the modern environmental movement decades ago? It was more than just new scientific insights or the dire predictions of a few die-hard activists. It was stories of birth defects and DDT-laced breast milk, things that cut right to the core of our natural concern for our own health and the health of our loved ones. It's just these kinds of stories that will inevitably energize and lend urgency to the mental environmental movement as well.

In 1996, social epidemiologists at Columbia University reported that more and more Americans are becoming depressed, that they are becoming depressed at a younger age, and that the severity and frequency of their depression is rising. They also found that people born after 1945 are ten times more likely to experience depression in their lives than people born before 1945.

noise

The World Health Organization has predicted that if mental dysfunction keeps rising at its current rate, then mental disease will be bigger than heart disease by the year 2020. Already, five of the ten leading causes of disability and premature death worldwide are psychiatric disorders.

adcreep

A factory dumps pollution into the water and air because that's the most efficient way to produce wood pulp or steel. A TV or radio station or magazine dispenses sex and violence and "pollutes" a culture because that's the most efficient way to produce audiences. It pays to pollute. The psychic fallout is just the cost of doing business.

In 1998, Rutgers University public health researcher William Vega found that recent Mexican emigrants to the US showed half the incidence of psychological dysfunction as their new American neighbours. After 13 years, however, their rates of depression, anxiety and drug use had almost doubled, to the point where they were on par with the average American's. Further studies have replicated and extended these findings, which leads us to an inevitable conclusion: there's something about American culture, like the culture of other affluent nations, that is making people sick.

TOXIC CULTURE

Right now, for each and every one of us living in the so-called "First World," a very personal, almost Faustian dilemma presents itself: What's the point of living in one of the most dynamic and affluent nations on Earth if we're feeling stressed and anxious all of the time? Have we gained our power and wealth at the price of – let's just say it – a piece of our soul? After thousands of years of struggling to survive, have we finally filled the hole in our stomachs, only to discover a new hole, one in our heads?

As the epidemic of mood disorders and other mental illnesses grows with each generation, it becomes ever more demanding to ignore. And the moment you confront the question head on, the cool, commercial façade of modern life suddenly cracks open. Behind it is a web of deeply intimate uncertainties. Why am I sad? Why am I anxious? Why can't I love? Why do I sense danger around every corner? Why am I so scared of dying? The answers are somewhere down in our collective subconscious, down through a postmodern hall of mirrors. And the trip looks foreboding.

And yet maybe, just maybe, this could be one of the most liberating journeys you'll ever take. Think of it as an existential whodunit, trying to solve the psycho-thriller of your life. Not only your life, in fact, but everyone's, since artists, designers and other public communicators are faced with an incredible, two-fold responsibility. First, we have to fess up to how we've contributed to the problem, with the images we've assembled, with the desires we've created, and with the products that we've made to sparkle. Then, we have to find ways to turn it all around.

Here goes:

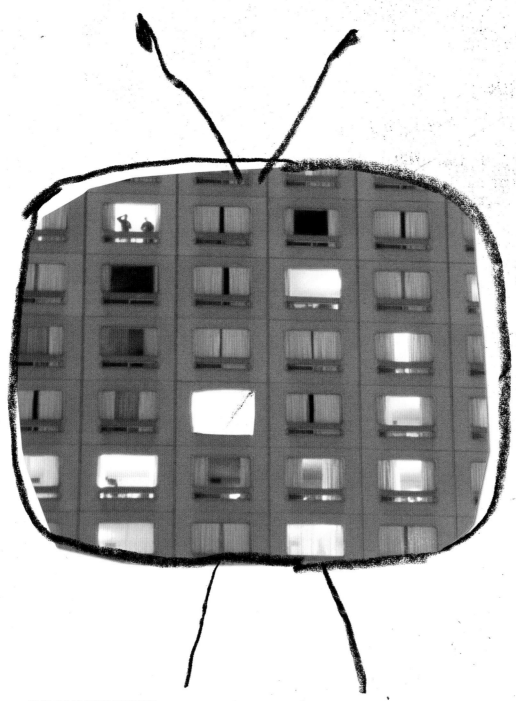

IS IT SEPARATION ANXIETY?

We stand at a pivotal moment in the human story. For 20,000 generations, our species lived in nature, taking our cues from the sky, the wind, the sea, the animals. We only entered into an electronic environment a generation or two ago. Now we're getting our cues from glowing screens. We watch nature shows instead of going venturing into the forest. We laugh at recorded jokes instead of joking around together and drool over internet porn instead of having actual sex. Slowly, we move toward a goal that Swiss author Max Frisch once described as "arranging the world so that we do not experience it."

IS IT SOCIAL ISOLATION?

Mood disorders like depression are much more common among people who live by themselves. They are more common still among the utter loners – folks living without any families, friends, or social support systems at all. In late capitalist societies, young people are expected to forsake the trades of their parents and to make a living as hyper-specialized free agents, leaving them to forge their own identities in a social vacuum. Researchers believe that this is one of the reasons why mood disorder rates are far higher in rich nations than in traditional societies, where extended families and intimate social networks are still the norm.

IS IT POST-TRAUMATIC SHOCK?

Those who have fallen victim to torture, who have witnessed horrific acts of violence and cruelty, who have seen unspeakable disaster, they tend to become paralyzed with the burden of those moments, reliving them over and over again beyond all reason. In times of warfare, it's referred to as shell shock. But what happens when we witness untold torture, mayhem, violence and cruelty – both real and imagined – every single day, on TV, in the movie theatre, on the pages of a newspaper, over the internet? What do we call our paralyzing fear then?

IS IT INFORMATION OVERLOAD?

There is more printed information in a Sunday edition of *The New York Times* than the average person living during the Renaissance would have encountered in a lifetime. The information glut, the so-called "data smog" hanging low in the valleys, calls to mind the bewildered student's lament: "I don't need to know any more – I already know more than I can understand." Information that arrives indiscriminately and is directed at no one in particular becomes a kind of psychic pollution. Lacking the capacity to sort through the crush of data, we are left with little means to judge what's useful, relevant or important. And so, although life has never been more exciting, more stimulating, there are widespread complaints of numbness, of blunted emotional response – as if the part of the forebrain that feels deeply has been saturated or stunned.

COMMERCIALIZED SCHOOLS

IS IT AFFLUENZA? CONSUMER CAPITALISM?

The paradox can be lost on no one. We are enjoying unprecedented prosperity – good health care, long life expectancy, secure food supplies, plenty of leisure and entertainment – and yet we can't seem to stay happy. Until relatively recently, the singular, all-consuming goal of most of us has been simply to keep on living, to find the next meal, to keep a roof over our heads, to protect ourselves from the cold and the heat and wind. It was grueling, back-breaking, incessant, but it did give us purpose. Now that we have more than we could ever need, we are left to search for something else to simulate the struggle. So we spend our time hunting for things we don't really need, and we call it shopping. Advertisers get into the act by assuring us that their products can make us whole again. But the relentless quest for money and consumer goods is just a pale stand-in, one that widens the gulf between ourselves and our communities, and in the end exacerbates our sense of having no purpose.

om

og

IS IT THE POMO ZEITGEIST?

Postmodernism is potentially the most
depressing philosophy ever to spring from
the human mind. Lost in the pomo hall of
mirrors, we suspect that we've reached an
endpoint in human history. The ceaseless
extension of the frontiers of creativity is
dead. Innovation is dead. Originality is
dead. The avant-garde artistic tradition is
dead. All religions and utopian political
visions are dead. And resistance to
the status quo is impossible because
revolution, too, is now impossible.
Like it or not, we humans are stuck in a
permanent crisis of meaning, a poorly lit
room from which there is no escape.

The holocaust-surviving psychologist
Victor Frankl identified patients caught
in what he called the "existential
vacuum." It is a spiritual affliction.
Your life feels utterly devoid of purpose.
No path beckons. Bit by bit, a paralytic
cynicism sets in. You believe in nothing.
You accept nothing as truthful, useful
or significant. You assign no value to
anything you're currently doing, and you
can't imagine doing anything of much
value in the future.

ADBUSTERS

JOURNAL OF THE MENTAL ENVIRONMENT >> MAY/JUN 2002 >> NO.41

Mad pride

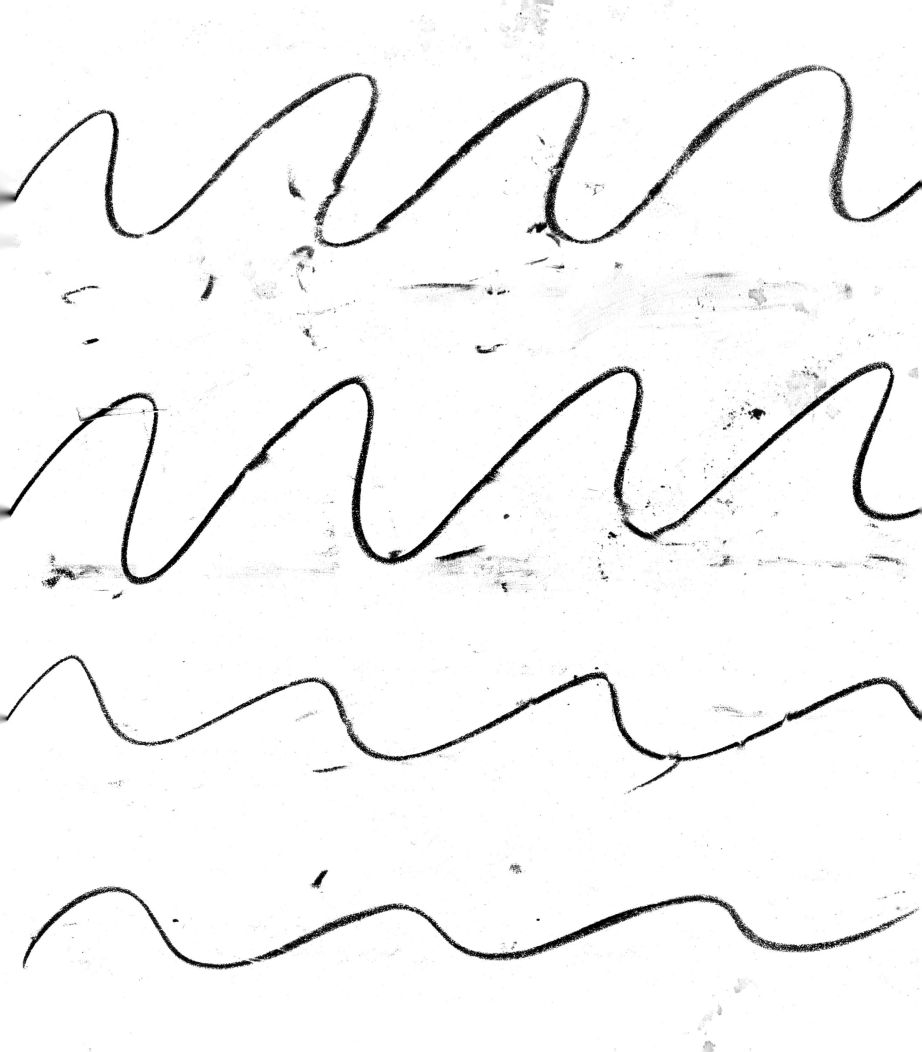

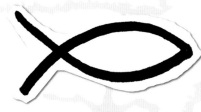

THE ECOLOGY OF MIND

After we crawled out of the sea, it took us thousands of generations to learn how to breathe the air and adapt to living on the land, our "natural environment." It's reasonable to assume that it will take us dozens of generations to adapt to the new, electronic environment that's rapidly replacing our "natural" one. The wild mood swings and the barely repressed anger may simply be symptoms of the shock our systems are experiencing. We are emerging evolutionary creatures, panting for breath on the electronic beach.

That beach is full of pitfalls and poisons that can do us in. What follows is the beginning of a new science, an enquiry into the nature of the psychic shocks we have to deal with daily – a survey of the threats to our ecology of mind.

NOISE

For most of human history the ambient noise was wind, rain, insects, birds, animals and people talking. Now the soundtrack of our lives is the hum of computers, the drone of appliances, the dull roar of traffic. Various kinds of noise – white, pink, brown, blue – are ever present. Trying to live your life above the noise of our wired world is like living next to a freeway: you get used to it, but at the cost of your mindfulness.

Less noise is what we need. Silence is to a healthy mind what clean air and water are to a healthy body. Long ago we learned to watch what we dump into our bodies; now we need to be equally careful about what we dump into our minds.

JOLTS

In broadcasting terms, a jolt is any "technical event" that interrupts the flow of sound or thought or imagery – a shift in camera angle, a gunshot, a cut to commercial, a flashing pop-up window. A jolt forces your mind to take notice and pump for meaning, even if there is none.

In 1978, when Jerry Mander first defined "technical events" in his book *Four Arguments for the Elimination of Television*, regular TV programming averaged ten technical events per minute, 20 during commercials. Twenty-five years later these figures have more than doubled. MTV now delivers 60 jolts per minute, and some viewers, still insufficiently stimulated, roam the channels for even more action.

Why are jolts and shocks so inherently compelling? The Russian psychologist Ivan Pavlov was among the first to try to explain this. Any change in stimulus releases hormones that trigger the biologically imbedded fight-or-flight response, left over from a time when survival depended on being alert to anything in the environment that happened at a faster-than-normal pace. The response arose to keep us from being eaten by cave bears. It did not arise to keep us glued to our TV sets or surfing the internet.

However, most TV programs are designed to do just that. They are scripted to deliver the maximum number of jolts per minute. When you watch TV, you are in fight-or-flight mode practically the whole time. Random violence and meaningless sex drop in out of the blue and without context.

That's pretty much the premise the commercial mass media has operated on ever since Mander's book. Keep the jolts and shocks coming. Keep audiences on the edge and sell their attention spans to the advertiser before they regain their bearings. What is a postmodern spectacle, after all, if not an array of carefully orchestrated jolts?

INFOTOXINS

The reality presented to us by the media always has a spin on it. Ads stretch the truth, news bites give only part of the story, and press releases are carefully tailored to make leaders look irreproachable. We are constantly being hyped, suckered and lied to. The marketers, spin doctors and PR agents that produce commercial and political propaganda realize what we as a society hate to admit: disinformation works.

Say that an overwhelming majority of respected scientists believe that human actions are causing potentially catastrophic climate change. As an auto-maker, we stand to lose out. So let's manipulate popular opinion by funding a handful of contrarians who believe otherwise. Then we launch a campaign to suggest that any threat to the car is an attack on personal freedoms. We fund "grassroots" groups to defend the right to drive. We portray anti-car activists as prudes who long for the days of the horse and buggy. We allow our disinformation to accumulate in the public imagination, just like mercury accumulates in an ecosystem. Once we've circulated enough of the toxin, the balance of public opinion will shift to our side. We sit back, watch our infotoxins spread – and get ready to sell bigger, badder cars for years to come.

Can civil society, ordinary citizens, come up with antidotes to the infotoxins and infoviruses spreading in our midst? The answer may depend on how much we've ingested of the most potent and persistent mental poison of them all: cynicism.

You reach down to pull your golf ball out of the hole and there, at the bottom of the cup, is an ad for a brokerage firm. You fill your car with gas, there's an ad on the nozzle. You wait for your bank machine to spit out money and an ad scrolls by in the little window. You drive through the countryside and your view of the fields is broken at intervals by enormous billboards. Your kids watch Pepsi and Snickers ads in the classroom (the school has made the devil's bargain of accepting free audio-visual equipment in exchange for airing these ads). You think you've seen it all, but you haven't. A US marketing firm announces plans to send an inflatable billboard adorned with corporate logos into geostationary orbit, viewable every night like a second moon. Software engineers demonstrate a program that turns your cursor into a corporate icon whenever you visit a commercial site. A Japanese schoolboy becomes a neon sign during his daily two-hour subway commute by wearing a battery-powered vest promoting an electronics giant. Administrators in a Texas school district announce plans to boost revenues by selling ad space on the roofs of the district's 17 schools – arresting the attention of the 58 million commercial jet passengers who fly into Dallas each year. A boy named David Bentley in Sydney, Australia, literally rents his head to corporate clients, shaving a new ad into his hair every few weeks ("I know for sure that at least 2,000 teenagers at my high school will read my head every day to see what it says," says the young entrepreneur, "I just wish I had a bigger head."). An American woman is paid $10,000 to tattoo the name of a casino on her forehead. You pick up a banana in the supermarket and there, on a little sticker, is an ad for the new summer blockbuster at the multiplex ("It's interactive because you have to peel them off," says one ad executive, "And people look at ten pieces of fruit before they pick one, so we get multiple impressions."). Boy Scouts in the UK sell corporate ad space on their merit badges. An Australian radio station dyes its logo on two million eggs. IBM beams its logo onto the clouds above San Francisco with a laser (the image is visible from 10 miles away). Bestfoods unveils plans to stamp its Skippy brand onto the crisp tabula rasa of a New Jersey beach each morning at low tide, where it will push peanut butter for a few hours before being washed by the waves. Coca-Cola strikes a six-month deal with the Australian postal service for the right to cancel stamps with a Coke ad. A company called VideoCart installs interactive screens on supermarket carts, so that you can see ads while you shop (a company executive calls the little monitors "the most powerful micromarketing medium available today."). In the 1990s, marketers began installing ad boards in men's washrooms on college campuses, at eye-level above the urinals. From an advertising executive's perspective, it was a brilliant coup: where else is a guy going to look? But from a cultural health perspective it is a tragedy of the mental commons.

THE TRAGEDY OF THE MENTAL COMMONS

DRIVING TO THE AIRPORT TO PICK UP A FRIEND, I STOP AT a red light. My eyes wander to a bus-stop bench across the intersection. "Norma Whitfield – Your Real-Estate Connection." Wham. Before I even have time to react, the advertisement has entered my mind and lodged itself between the folds of my thoughts. Another chunk of my mental landscape, grabbed without consent. There was nothing special about this ad. Every bench in the city is festooned with a marketing message, and my eyes have passed over thousands, possibly millions, like it before. Yet this time it stood out, as if some balance inside me had tipped, and I suddenly felt saturated.

Thirty-five years ago, Garret Hardin, a professor at the University of California, Santa Barbara, authored a ground-breaking article in the journal *Science* that introduced an idea: the tragedy of the commons. Our survival was at stake, he argued, if we failed to open our eyes and realize that Earth's physical resources were finite. Treating them as a free-for-all was no longer acceptable if we wanted to reduce human suffering and prolong our existence on this planet.

To illustrate the tragedy, he used the example of fourteenth-century common land. "Picture a pasture open to all," he wrote. "It is to be expected that each herdsman will try to keep as many cattle as possible on the commons." When a herder adds a cow to the pasture, he reaps the benefit of a larger herd. Meanwhile, the cost of the animal – the damage done to the pasture – is divided among all the herdsmen. This continues until, finally, the herders reach a delicate point: as the pasture becomes overgrazed, each new animal threatens the well-being of the entire herd. "At this point," Hardin argues, "the inherent logic of the commons remorselessly generates tragedy."

For me, the advertisement on the bus-stop bench felt like that tragic breach. We continue to share a commons today – a commons of the mind. At every level this mental commons is cluttered and commercialized. Millions of data points and marketing messages threaten to "overgraze" our attention. Our mind is their pasture.

"Ruin is the destination toward which all men rush," said Hardin. As pessimistic as this view is, we have proved him right. Since he penned this warning, humanity has spread to every corner of the globe: we've scoured the land, razed the forests, emptied the seas and dirtied the rivers in the selfish interest of progress. Now, just as we begin to grasp our impact on the physical commons, the tragedy has begun to replay itself in an even more fragile realm. The assault on the mental environment has become an ever greater threat to our survival: we are losing our capacity to focus, to think,

to find common ground, to communicate and come to agreement. We are losing the mental clarity to deal with the crises that we have created.

An exaggeration, you say? Not quite. The staggering rise of anxiety and attention deficit disorders, depression, suicide, workplace violence and addiction is now a staple story of our news media. Less familiar is the concern rippling through the marketing industry itself. The herders are getting nervous: "Marketers are going through a difficult period right now," declares one company's website. "Channel proliferation, attention span reduction and marketing overload are creating an increasingly cynical consumer audience who are each subjected to over one million marketing messages per year (or over 3,000 per day). 'If you're not interesting me now, then you can forget later,' is becoming their mantra." In a desperate attempt to free our mindspace, we are simply tuning out of everything around us – flipping channels during commercials, staring right past billboards, and ignoring banner ads on websites.

Even the "well-adjusted" among us are feeling the pressure. The effects may be subtle – a slight anxiety, a cynical attitude, a wave of fear – but this makes them all the more insidious. You see a can of Coke in a movie, and you stop following the plot to deconstruct Coke's marketing strategy and determine that you've just been subjected to paid product placement. You see a kid in a bandana loitering in a convenience store parking lot, and a flood of mental images and messages warns you that he may be a gang member. Instead of working, you check your e-mail every ten minutes in need of new information, fresh stimulus. You notice that you can't speak or listen for more than a minute anymore.

Is it too late to reclaim our mental commons? It wasn't long ago that our mindspace was still comparatively clean. I can remember – and I'm only 30 – when bus benches were only for sitting on, when the wall above the urinal was just an expanse of white tile, when a fashion magazine was lighter than a phone book. Would it be that hard to get it back?

The question, as Hardin noted, is one of freedom. "When men mutually agreed to pass laws against robbing, mankind became more free, not less so." We must decide whose freedom is more important: the bank robber's or the banker's; the marketer's or our own. We need to grasp the idea of the mental commons, and realize that it, too, can succumb to an all-too-human tragedy. Putting more cows out to pasture isn't helping anyone.

Kevin Arnold

CULTURAL DIVERSITY

When one corporation gains control of almost half of a country's information delivery systems (as is the case in Canada, for example), or amasses a global media empire the size of Rupert Murdoch's, the scope of public discourse shrinks and democracy suffers. When a handful of megacorporations control not only the daily newspapers and TV airwaves, but the magazine, book publishing, motion picture, home video and music industries as well, then cultural diversity plummets. When half a dozen giant corporations control half of all the news and entertainment flows around the planet, it is a cultural tragedy of monumental proportions.

INFODIVERSITY

Corporate control of culture has graver consequences than the same hairstyles, catchphrases, music and action-hero-antics being perpetrated ad nauseum around the world. In all systems, homogeneity is poison. Lack of diversity leads to inefficiency and failure. The loss of a language, tradition or heritage – or the forgetting of one good idea – is as big a loss to future generations as a biological species going extinct. Infodiversity is every bit as critical to our long-term survival as biodiversity. Both are bedrocks of human existence. Without both of them, a sane, sustainable future is unthinkable.

At a recent *Adbusters* office party, two young guys walked in the door, grabbed a beer and went straight to the computers, where they stayed for two hours. Except for a few minutes here and there when people came up behind them and commented on something, they had no social interaction whatsoever. I know these guys. They are very bright. They'd score way up there on an IQ test. But I wondered how they'd score on the Unreality Index (UI): the ratio of time spent in a virtual vs. a "real" environment. This ratio would be easy enough to calculate. You jot down the number of times a day you laugh at real jokes with real people in real situations against the number of times you laugh at media-generated jokes; the number of times you flirt or have real sex against the number of sexual hits you get from TV, magazines and the Internet. Then you tally up the numbers at the end of the week.

A NEW SCIENCE

If we learned how to measure the psychological impact of mental pollutants like jolts, shocks, and infotoxins on our minds, perhaps we could pioneer a new science of the ecology of mind. Perhaps, as this discipline progressed, we could establish safe pollution levels for our minds similar to the parts-per-billion environmental safety standards we have for our bodies. And maybe we could learn how to measure the psychological risks posed by living in different kinds of mental environments: living in Mumbai vs. living in Geneva, raising your kids in a big city vs. raising them in a small country town, being a painter vs. being a graphic designer.

We could then arrive at a Livability Index (LI) more revealing than the current indices that simply measure greenspace, smog levels and the quality of schools. With reliable Mental Environmental Indices (MEI), we could rate TV programs, films, and TV networks in terms of how many jolts per hour they manufacture, how much clutter they dump into the public mind and how this may be affecting our mental health.

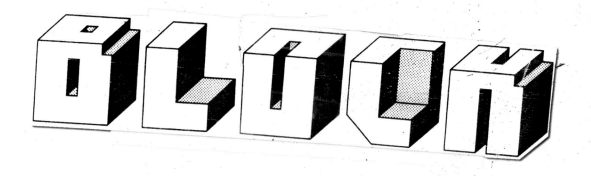

BLOCK

technique ~~sucks my~~ soul

sucks my

surface is all that counts.

.... things have really
gotten out of hand... I've become a feinschmecker, a
massager, a dilletante... I push tid bits of information around computer screens until what I'm working
on accumulates a kind of slickness... ....
....

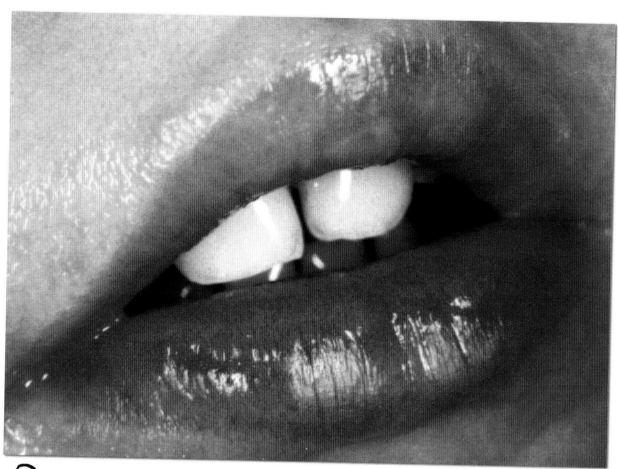

Perfectionism is a malignant force in our society

by the surface of things. The revelation of the inner, hidden, unconscious, dark reality of the world, which Wall himself often describes in his texts and statements as a universal economic law, does not occur here. The control to which the figures are subjected is twofold: by the artistic tradition and by the technical, photographic process. There is no room left for any additional determination which could itself be observed and critically opposed in reality.

Nevertheless, Wall's works have a public, liberating effect. The light of enlightenment, passing through what exists, does not encounter an opaque, dark core of reality,

This tastiness cannot be carried even by both hands.

For people who want their
straight lines to be straight,
life itself is the problem.
— Natalia Ilyin

Mirror.   Change what's on the surface.   Denied. Restricted.

"I want gaiety, friends, LOVE," she sobbed

"And you shall have them," I promised her

INTO a psychiatrist's chambers streams an endless tide of life's misfits. The lonely . . . the bitter . . . the repressed . . . the misunderstood.

And now before me stood yet another. I was certain, and later examination proved me right, that there was nothing organically wrong with her. Her face, her body, bloomed with beauty and vitality. Yet, emotionally, she was at the breaking point.

Gently, I probed for her history. She was 28, single, college bred, lived in a good home with parents of some means, but was definitely of the recluse type.

"Men friends?"

Her lips quivered as she leaned close to me. The flood-tide of her emotions burst through the gates of her control.

"You've hit on it, doctor, I'm lonely . . . desperately lonely," she sobbed. "Every girl I know is married, but no man seems to want *me*. They come—they go—I cannot hold them. Even my women friends seem to avoid me. I go nowhere . . . see no one. And, oh doctor, I want gaiety, friends, admiration, love . . . love . . . love."

She had risen; her face was almost against mine. In that instant I knew I had spotted the cause of her trouble. It was obvious.

But never in all my years of practice did I face a harder task than that of telling this unhappy girl the simple truth.* But tell her I did.

Today she is one of the happiest and most popular girls in our little city, and soon will marry a well-to-do Easterner who simply adores her.

Why Risk It?

Nothing is so fatal to friendships and romance as *halitosis (bad breath). No one is immune. And the insidious thing about halitosis is that you yourself never know when you have it; never realize when you are offending.

Why run the risk at all? All you need do to make your breath sweeter, purer, more wholesome and agreeable to others is to rinse the mouth with Listerine Antiseptic. This amazing deodorant halts food fermentation in the oral cavity, a major cause of breath odors; then overcomes the odors themselves. And it's so delightful to use.

Get in the habit of using Listerine Antiseptic night and morning, and between times before business or social engagements. It pays rich dividends in popularity.

LISTERINE *for* HALITOSIS

I love you,

Green Bay Packer Forrest Gregg. Photograph by Robert Riger, 1960 (courtesy of James Danziger Gallery)

[P 125 All American: A Style Book by Tommy Hilfiger]

INSERT COM

MERCI

FCUKINKYBUGGER

CHAPTER 6

POLITICO

s.11 — the affluent of the world circle their wagons in disbelief

darker

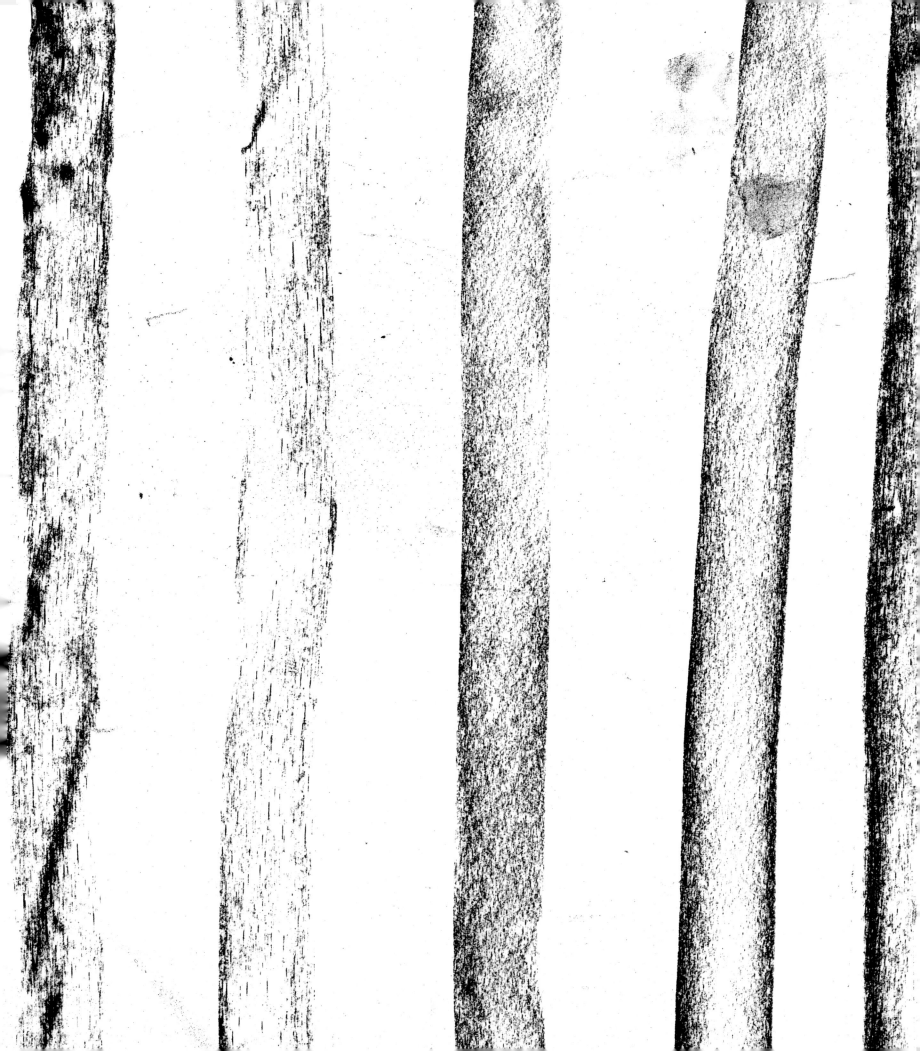

WIN A SUZUKI MOTORCYCLE!

★ **DRILL**

MISS USA!

DRILL exclusive:
The American beauty's
sexiest photos ever!

BOUNTY HUNTER'S BLUES

He fought the
law – guess
who won?

PLUS!

LEANN RIMES
ADAM CAROLLA
JORDAN LADD
NELLY VS. ZIMMER!
LINGERIE BOWL BABES!
SCARLETT JOHANSSON
CRICKET IN COMPTON!

SMACK DOWN!

The **XXXVIII**
bone-crunchingest
moments in sports!

WISEGUY WORKOUT

A former mobster
enters the Fitness
Protection Program

TOBY KEITH

Shocks y'all with
a soldier's song

SUSIE CASTILLO
MISS USA

JAN./FEB. 2004 $3.95 US $4.99 CAN

0 1>

7 25274 58253 2

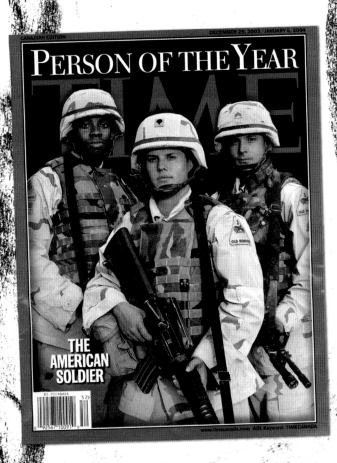

OUR CRISIS IS
A CRISIS OF
AESTHETICS

"Abstraction" opens up the prospect of an art that, following in the footsteps of pure philosophical inquiry, symphonic music, and certain expressions of spirituality, finds in geometry not only the new vernacular of the era of industry but also the secret language of the psyche or of the world, or of the psyche as world; an art that is "abstract" inasmuch as it has withdrawn from the realm of appearances stands in the pursuit of something anticipating the noumenal.

. . . purest idea . . . purest expression . . . eyes unclouded by the vulgarity of life . . . a universal language beyond the

It was at an exhibition of Russian art. I saw it from a distance at first: Kasimir Malevich's unmistakable, iconic *Black Square* – that perfect and immutable monolith, that palate-cleansing cipher which admits nothing but its own abstract purity. As I greedily approached it, I saw something that I never expected: variation. This was not the mathematical gesture of flawlessness that I had been holding in my mind for decades. This was messy, blotchy, even painterly, with rough-hewn edges.

everyday . . . feeling the caress of the transcendent . . . a whiff of the sublime . . . revealing totality, for all to behold . . .

This seedling protected by the House Chiefs for countless generations.

Arrival of whites.

what is abstraction?

a utopian realm of pure form
universality of expression, of emotion, of thought
the hue of infinity
a glimpse into the spiritual structure of nature itself
the culmination of thousands of years of human aesthetics

a fear of death
the loss of empathy
an escape from nature
a form of ecocide through willful ignorance
the incestuous victory of the single-minded logic freak
the fatal flaw of Western civilization

Mark Tansey's *Purity Test*, painted in response to Robert Smithson's emblematic *Spiral Jetty*, a massive earthwork constructed in 1970 in Utah's Great Salt Lake.

The evolution of western aesthetics is one of creeping abstraction – a turning away from the natural world.

the frozen empathy

Modernism gave birth to abstraction in a fit of dread, a paroxysm of fear born in the unpredictable dead of night, in the threatening wilderness, in the aftershock of an earthquake, in the bloodied trenches of a World War. The Futurists, the Constructivists, the Bauhaus – all of them were ruled by the tantalizing image of standing victorious over the trees, the mountains, and the sun itself. To tame an insane and corrupt world, they had to perfect it with logic. To tame art, they had to make paint do what it doesn't like to do without a fight.

This instinct still rules over us. But it does not have to be this way. Design doesn't need to be terrified, precious, idealized, sanitized. It can be visceral, messy, chaotic, anarchic. We can move on from the modernist impulse.

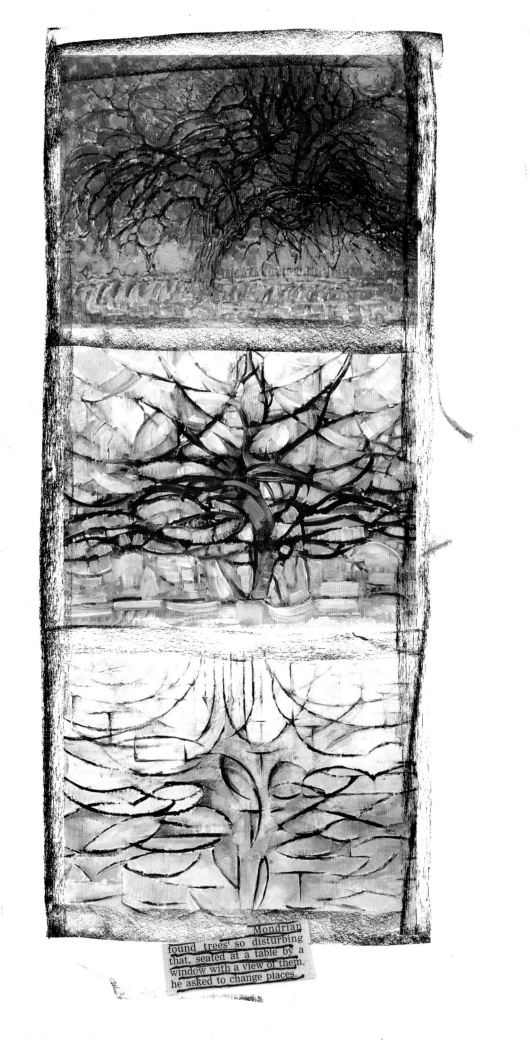

Mondrian found trees so disturbing that, seated at a table by a window with a view of them, he asked to change places.

I remember an encounter that I had with a group of young Japanese students in 1965. While discussing a book on European art history, we turned to a picture of Jesus on the cross. They were stunned, speechless. They shook their heads in amazement. "This cannot be a god," they said, "he looks too much like a loser to be a god."

the chilling emotional distance

They have kind eyes. They are good people. They invite me into their cozy, unassuming homes. I have no trouble getting along with them. I enjoy their company. I can even forget, if I so decide, about the hideous nature of their crimes. I could forget indefinitely if not for their hospitality, which strangely compels them to present the evidence, to display it on their dinner tables, to offer it to me on the end of forks. So natural have their crimes become that they hide the corpses of their dismembered victims behind nothing more elaborate than a bit of plastic wrap or waxed paper.

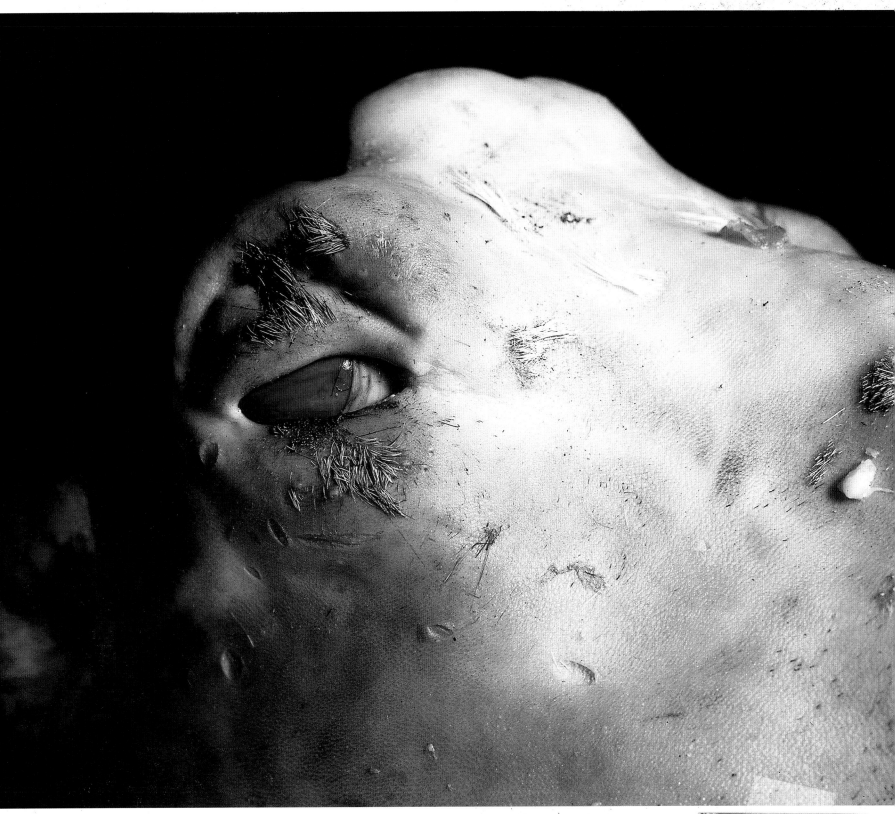

I find the thought of stuffing fragments of corpses down my throat quite repulsive, and I am amazed that so many people do it every day.

— Coetzee

Who is more brutal? The suicide bomber? The soldier who castrates his enemy and leaves him bleeding in the dirt? Or the political leaders who sign off on the cluster bombs that shred and maim tens of thousands?

In war, the passive God is forgotten. The self-sacrificing God – the God that finds strength in suppleness and suffering – does not suit our purposes. We want the active God, the masculine God, the red-blooded, take-no-prisoners God of brutish muscle.

prisoner of war, brutalized and left to die

183. **Ed Ruscha.** *Standard Station, Amarillo, Texas.* 1963. Oil on canvas, 64⅞" × 10'1¾" (164.8 × 309.2 cm). Hood Museum of Art, Dartmouth College, Hanover, New Hampshire. Gift of James J. Meeker, Class of 1958, in memory of Lee English [p 346 HI/LO]

The Brillo and Ketchup Boxes were also obvious parodies of the modular structures of Minimalist sculptors such as Carl Andre and Donald Judd. In finding the aesthetic of the avant-garde in the dated banalities of the storeroom, Warhol made somewhat the same point Lichtenstein had made with the sneaker sole, about the futility of trying to quarantine pure form and crass reference from each other. But the Minimalist aesthetic was not just a generic form of abstraction; it involved a specific range of manmade materials, and a sensibility of materialist austerity, that separated it from the idealizing abstract art of earlier modernism. Moreover, in paintings such as Frank Stella's black-stripe canvases, and in sculptures as diverse as Dan Flavin's fluorescent tubes or Carl Andre's metal plaques, Minimalism permitted a variable range of feelings (pristinely clinical rationality, or brute, raw power, or imposing theatricality, or brash opulence, to cite only a few); and its use of clarified, impersonal standardization could serve an artist as an adjustable lens rather than just an immovable template. Ed Ruscha's *Standard Station, Amarillo, Texas* (fig. 183), for example, was—no less than the Soup Cans and Brillo Boxes— knowingly fixed on the reductivist aesthetics of its day, and involved in partial parody of hard-edge abstract painting. Yet its emotional response to the encounter of that aesthetic with the look of mass society is wholly different.

Where Warhol and Lichtenstein made a salutary regression into the world of cheap, coarse printing, Ruscha effected a smoother segue between basic art-school graphic technique and a personal poetics. When he included material similar to that of New York Pop, such as a comic or a Spam can, he isolated these things in fields of color, enlarging the detached logos to assume a classic rectitude, while leaving the trashy querulousness of the object itself to plead against the cool, clean silence (fig. 184). Like others before him, Ruscha found a landscape that made him a painter; in his case it involved an interlock between the expanse of the Western deserts or the Pacific vista and the blandness of "modernized" commercial design. In works like *Standard Station*, Ruscha finds his Minimalism not along the K-Mart shelves, but out where the commercial template of clean, neat invariance falls into synchronization with a landscape of endless anonymity—primary-colored plastic evenly illuminated against empty sky. The modular, mechanical rhythm of Warhol is here translated into an extended, imperturbable continuity, and repetitious crowding is replaced by remote loneliness. Here also the fake promotional rhetoric of colossal grandeur—the plunging forced perspective of the gas station image—meets the reality of the country's scale. The odd alchemy that Ruscha sees and conveys is that a specificity arises from the meeting of two seemingly generic absolutes: a set of

346

If I don't photograph this, people like my mom
will think war is what they SEE ON T.V.
–Kenneth Jarecke, photojournalist

all these things
are to be answered for!

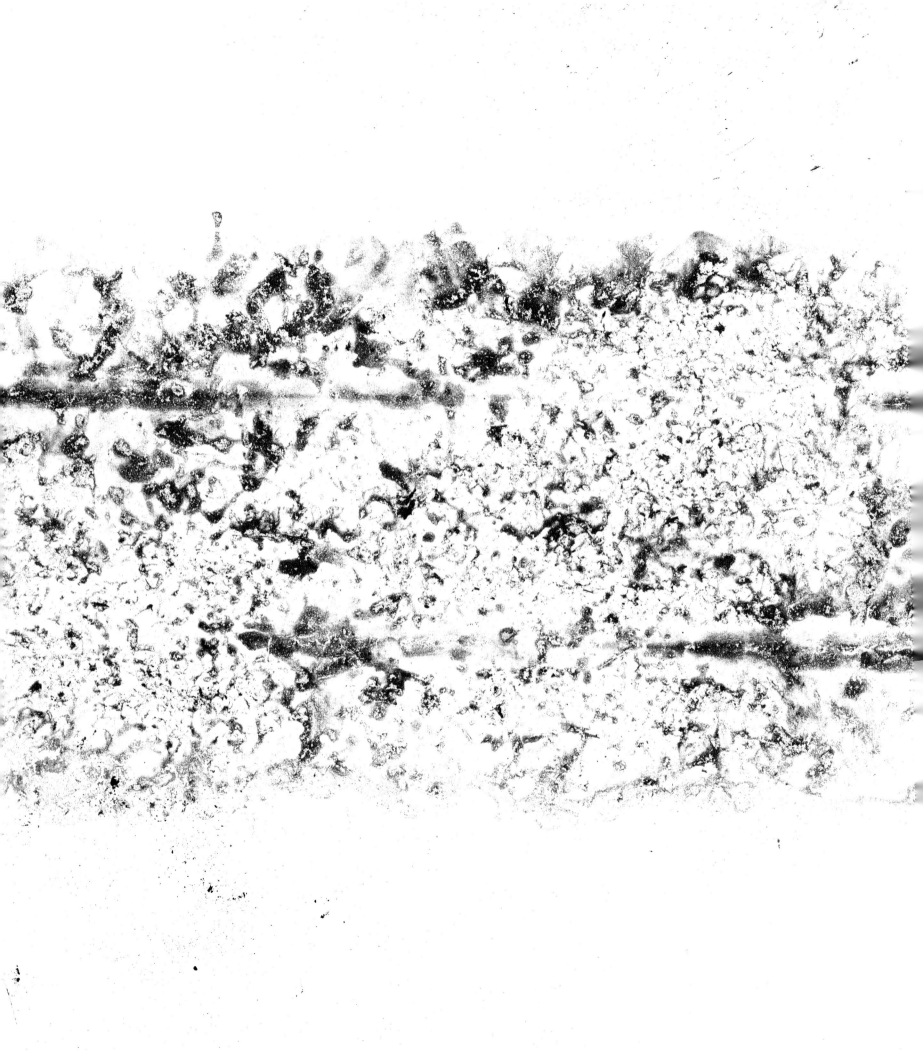

to believe
in this world,
in this life,
has become my
most difficult task

IT'S TIME FOR A RADICAL RE-THINK.

GERT DUMBAR

each day do something
that won't compute

- ROUGHER CLOTHES - not that same old black

I locate myself in a relatively open space – a low hill is
particularly good, or a wide field. I relax a bit, take a few breaths, gaze
around. Then I close my eyes and let myself begin to feel the whole bulk of my
past – the whole mass of events leading up to this very moment. And I call into
awareness, as well, my whole future – all those projects and possibilities that lie
waiting to be realized. I imagine this past and this future as two cast balloons of time,
separated from each other like bulbs of an hourglass, yet linked together at the single
moment where I stand pondering them. And then, very slowly, I allow both of these immense
bulbs of time to begin leaking their substance into this minute moment between them, into the
present. Slowly, imperceptibly at first, the present moment begins to grow. Nourished by the leakage
from the past and the future, the present moment swells in proportion as those other dimensions
shrink. Soon it is very large; and the past and future have dwindled down to mere knots on the edge
of this huge expanse. At this point I let past and the future dissolve entirely.
And I open my eyes.

— Abram

silence
I liked the way it sounded

I lived with constant noise from TVs, traffic and
stereos. Then I tried something new – silence.
I liked the way it sounded.

Silence calmed me down, lifted my mood and
helped me focus on what was really important.

Now I understand why so many people say
silence is sacred.

Try it.

what does
design
look like
after all
commercial/ego
pretensions
have been
stripped
away?

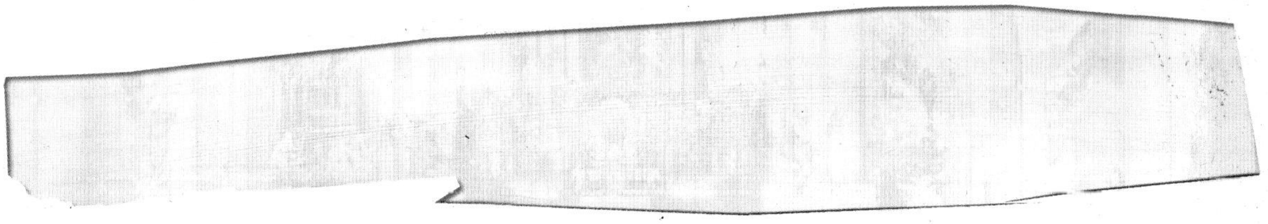

nature is closed out.. An entirely man-made experience is created.

the tyranny of straight lines and "right" angles

a house is not a form, but a process

I was leafing through a coffee-table book when Frank Lloyd's "Falling Water" house caught my eye. I'd seen it many times before – the bold clean lines, the subdued colors, the oriental mystique – but this time, for some strange reason, instead of seeing the house, I saw the rocks, the trees, the ferns, the shrubs. I heard the rush of water, felt the roots wriggling in the ground, the sap moving up the trees, the sunlight penetrating the leaves. As my imagination wandered, I even caught a glimpse of the myriad patterns in the snowflakes that would fall here tonight.

At some point in your life, you have to come to terms with the fact that, in just about every way, nature is a much better designer than you are.

THE STRAIGHT LINE IS GODLESS AND IMMORAL. — Friedensreich Hundertwasser

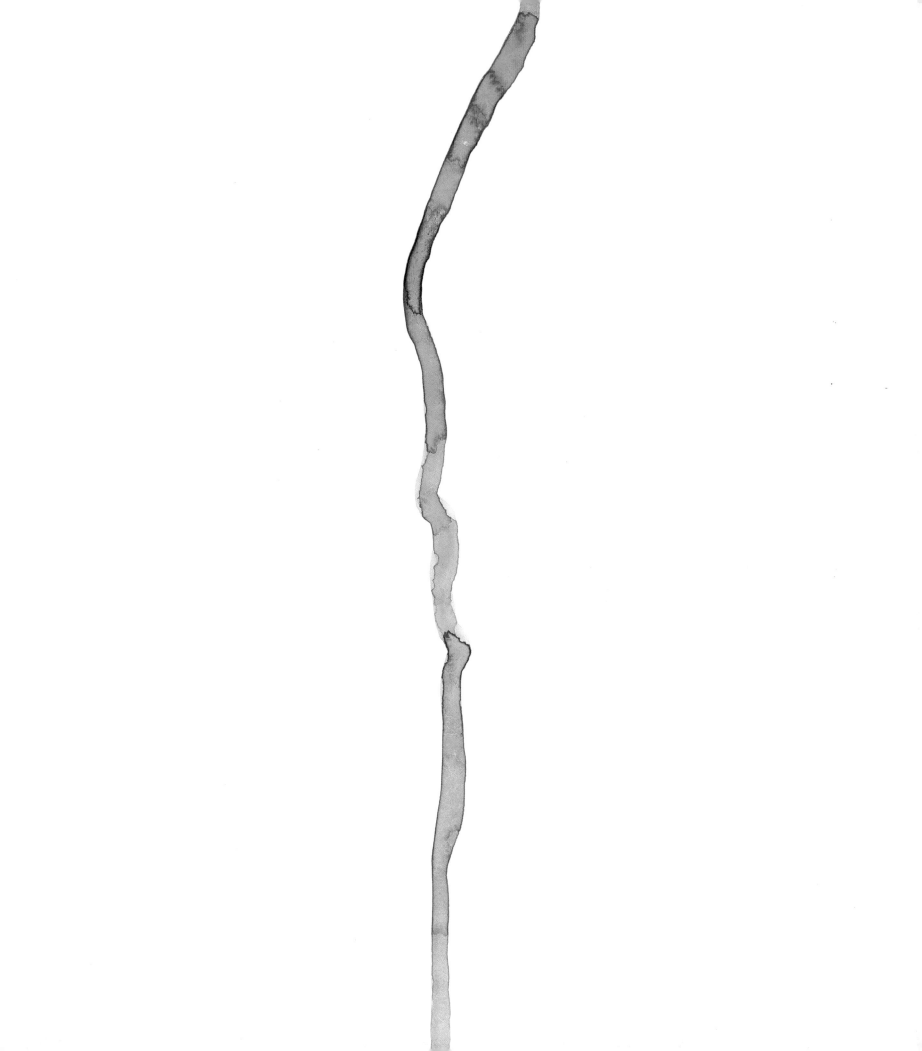

When I saw it, my heart fell. A good Tea-bowl, yes, but how ordinary! So simple, no more ordinary thing could be imagined. There is no trace of ornament, not a trace of calculation. It is just a Korean food bowl, a bowl, moreover, that a poor man would use every day — commonest crockery.

The clay had been dug from the hill at the back of the house; the glaze was made from the ash from the hearth; the potter's wheel had been irregular. The shape revealed no particular thought: it was one of many. The work had been fast; the turning was rough, done with dirty hands; the throwing slipshod; the glaze had run over the foot. The throwing room had been dark. The kiln was a wretched affair; the firing careless. Sand had stuck to the pot, but nobody minded; no one invested the thing with any dreams.

More than anything else, this pot is healthy. Made for a purpose, made to do work. Sold to be used in everyday life. If it were fragile, it would not serve its purpose.

It is not made with thought to display effects of detail, so there is no time for the disease of technical elaboration to creep in. It is not inspired by theories of beauty, so there is no occasion for it to be poisoned by over-awareness. There is nothing in it to justify inscribing it with the maker's name. No optimistic ideals gave it birth, so it cannot become the plaything of sentimentality. It is not the product of nervous excitement, so it does not harbour the seeds of perversion. It was created with a very simple purpose, so it shuns the world of brilliance and colour.

The Tea masters assert that Korean bowls are the best. It is an honest admittance. Why, one asks, do they surpass Japanese bowls? And the answer is that Japanese potters strove to make good pots according to accepted canons or rules. To confuse the two approaches, that of the maker and that of the user, is quite wrong. Production was poisoned by appreciation. Japanese bowls bear the scars of awareness. Raku Chojiro, Honami Koetsu, and other individual potters all to a greater or lesser degree suffer from this sickness. It is all very well to find irregularities of form in Ido bowls charming, but to make pots with deliberate distortions is to immediately lose that charm. If glazes skip during the firing of a pot, it is natural, it may be a blessing in disguise, but deliberately to cause it to do so with the misguided idea of following some Tea master's rules is quite another matter.

THE UNKNOWN CRAFTSMAN - A JAPANESE INSIGHT INTO BEAUTY
by Soetsu Yanagi
Kodansha 1972

Every Ido bowl has the look
of having attained Buddahood

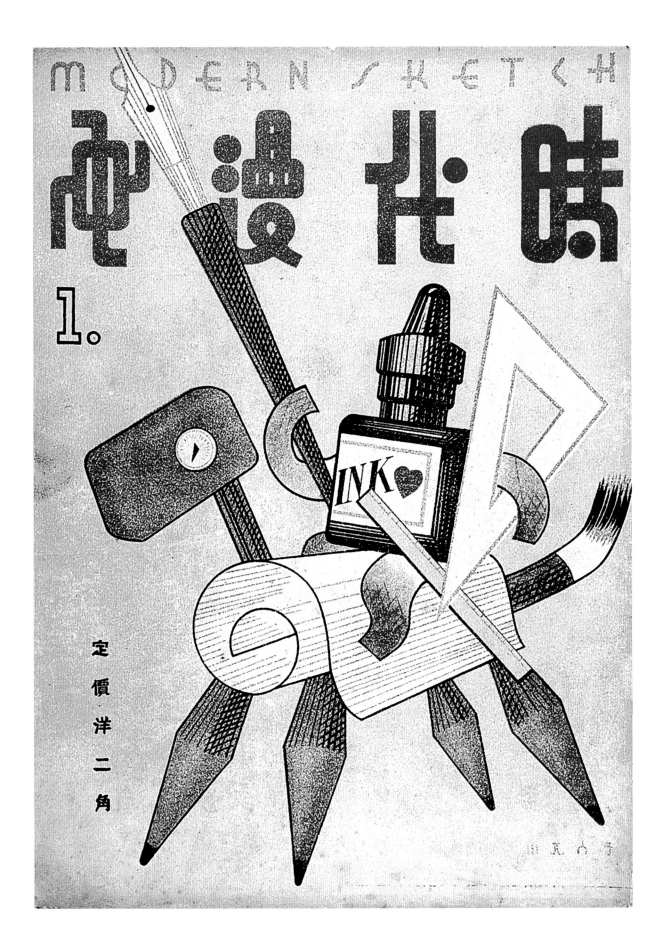

First Things First Manifesto

We, the undersigned, are graphic designers, art directors and visual communicators who have been raised in a world in which the techniques and apparatus of advertising have persistently been presented to us as the most lucrative, effective and desirable use of our talents. Many design teachers and mentors promote this belief; the market rewards it; a tide of books and publications reinforces it.

Encouraged in this direction, designers then apply their skill and imagination to sell dog biscuits, designer coffee, diamonds, detergents, hair gel, cigarettes, credit cards, sneakers, butt toners, light beer and heavy-duty recreational vehicles. Commercial work has always paid the bills, but many graphic designers have now let it become, in large measure, *what graphic designers do.* This, in turn, is how the world perceives design. The profession's time and energy is used up manufacturing demand for things that are inessential at best.

Many of us have grown increasingly uncomfortable with this view of design. Designers who devote their efforts primarily to advertising, marketing and brand development are supporting, and implicitly endorsing, a mental environment so saturated with commercial messages that it is changing the very way citizen-consumers speak, think, feel, respond and interact. To some extent we are all helping draft a reductive and immeasurably harmful code of public discourse.

There are pursuits more worthy of our problem-solving skills. Unprecedented environmental, social and cultural crises demand our attention. Many cultural interventions, social marketing campaigns, books, magazines, exhibitions, educational tools, television programs, films, charitable causes and other information design projects urgently require our expertise and help.

We propose a reversal of priorities in favor of more useful, lasting and democratic forms of communication — a mindshift away from product marketing and toward the exploration and production of a new kind of meaning. The scope of debate is shrinking; it must expand. Consumerism is running uncontested; it must be challenged by other perspectives expressed, in part, through the visual languages and resources of design.

In 1964, 22 visual communicators signed the original call for our skills to be put to worthwhile use. With the explosive growth of global commercial culture, their message has only grown more urgent. Today, we renew their manifesto in expectation that no more decades will pass before it is taken to heart.

Jonathan Barnbrook
Nick Bell
Andrew Blauvelt
Hans Bockting
Irma Boom
Sheila Levrant de Bretteville
Max Bruinsma
Siân Cook
Linda van Deursen
Chris Dixon
William Drenttel
Gert Dumbar
Simon Esterson
Vince Frost
Ken Garland
Milton Glaser
Jessica Helfand
Steven Heller
Andrew Howard
Tibor Kalman
Jeffery Keedy
Zuzana Licko
Ellen Lupton
Katherine McCoy
Armand Mevis
J. Abbott Miller
Rick Poynor
Lucienne Roberts
Erik Spiekermann
Jan van Toorn
Teal Triggs
Rudy VanderLans
Bob Wilkinson

NO MORE KISSING CORPORATE ASS

I am not a decorator, a packager...
I am the author, the storyteller,
the creator of meaning

- wipe the slate clean
- wipe out the past and present
- clear the space for something else
- declare a new beginning
- Start a new period of experimentation
  craziness
  ~~█████████~~
  trying new things

I vow:

from now on, I swear off corporate --> human
communication and plunge into the most intimate
kind of human --> human communication

AN ENTIRELY NEW
DESIGN IS POSSIBLE

and there's green ones and there's blue ones and there's red ones and there's yellow ones and they all live in little boxes little homes all the same

you break out of the commercial design box and start playing around with the eco- and psycho-dimensions of the product-in-use

As the planet degrades,

a new meaning, a new aesthetic emerges.

 **ADBUSTERS**

PSYCHO-DESIGN CONTEST

We're looking for theoretical and practical works that transcend the current commercial paradigm. We're looking for designs that speak to their users, even snap at their fingers. As Stefane Barbeau has noted, "Design is traditionally driven by aesthetic, functional, production and market factors. What if suddenly these parameters were grossly distorted, or even removed entirely?" The result would be psycho-design.

The rules are simple. Take everything you know about design and throw it out. Try a different tack. Instead of obsessing on the glitz, the saleability, the cool of the object you're designing, think about other psychological states your designs might induce. Instead of increasing desire, try reducing it. Instead of saving time, s-t-r-e-t-c-h it. Forget about planned obsolescence and start designing products to last a hundred years.

In most cases, the unsustainable element of a product is not the product per se, but rather the product-in-use – that is, most of the damage that consumer products cause to people, to communities and to the environment arises from the way in which products are used and abused by consumers. We must focus on this product-in-use dimension of design.

Psycho-design is where the tire hits the road, where design hits reality. It's the moment when a thousand men take out your razor, toss the packaging, glance in your mirror, turn on your tap, and scrape the blade against their skin. It's the percent of them who leave the tap running. It's the number who consider switching to non-disposables, or who consider growing beards instead. For daydreaming desk-jockeys in the pixel-pushing trade, psycho-design is a much-deserved relief from the heartbreak of commercialism, a chance to start playing with the psychological dimensions of the product-in-use.

WHAT TO SEND: Sketches, photos, blueprints, etc.

WHERE TO SEND:
artdirector@adbusters.org

WHEN TO SEND IT: Before the big crash.

slow sipper

create new ambiences & psychic possibilities

hand knitted

soothing color

slips on easy

No, it's not to keep the TV warm. Put the ugly roommate under wraps and you'll find yourself in a strange sort of pact – who dares to ruin every conversation and derail every thought by letting the beast back out again?

you sit, you wobble, you understand

The not-so-gentle reminder of your sedentary lifestyle. Like a skateboard or a bicycle, using the seat eventually becomes second nature, but not without preliminary experimentation – and risk. Take it for granted, take a nasty spill. Not up to the challenge? Then go for a walk.

inhibit impulse
scramble habits
modulate desire

DARKSWITCH
Jarrod Beglinger

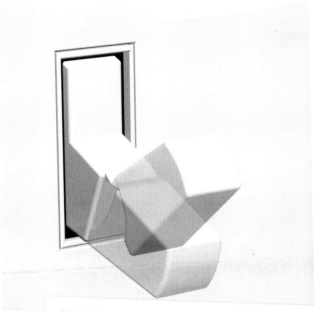

What's with this switch-on-a-hinge that's easy to turn off, but hard to turn on? A light bulb goes on in your head: DarkSwitch is bringing consciousness to kilowatt consumption. One of six available designs.

VEGANBONES
Stefane Barbeau, Ryan McManus

VeganBones are ceramic substitutes for vegetarians who hunger for bone-based cuisine. Stuffed with faux meat or pressed into tofu, they rekindle fond memories of BBQ ribs, rack of lamb, hot chicken wings or drumsticks. Smother 'em with sauce.

instead of making it easier, you make it harder

The eternity faucet is an indoor-plumbing memory of the labour-intensive village water pump. The handle is small, smooth and hard to turn. The colour – emergency red – is a heads-up that wasting water is a deadly game.

Why is it called the eternity faucet? To give you something to think about as you wait for the water to trickle from the tiny, aerated spout.

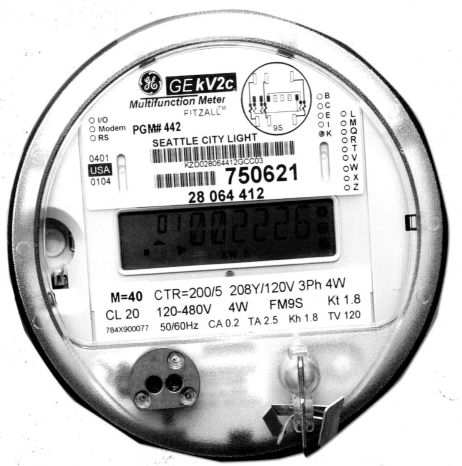

you make waste visible

The manager of a housing co-op was increasingly frustrated with her tenants. No matter how much she reminded and badgered them, no matter how many meetings she convened, no matter how much goodwill there was for the task, the tenants would not, could not reduce their energy consumption. Finally she hit an idea. What would happen, she wondered, if the electricity meters were moved from the basement to a conspicuous spot right beside the front door, so that each time the tenants left or entered their home they could see how fast their meter was whirring?

The meters were moved. Lo and behold, within a few weeks electricity consumption fell 30 percent.

Carbonometer

Rest assured that a team of brilliant designers and engineers has massaged every last nook, cranny, curve, handle and sparkle on your automobile, and that another team of whip-smart talent birthed the ads that convinced you to buy it. At the same time, wrestle with the fact that those beautiful minds, perhaps inadvertently, have created and sold the worst product ever to curse the planet, a noisy, dirty, sprawl-inducing, climate-changing monstrosity. The average car produces five tonnes of carbon dioxide and other greenhouse gases each year – a number most of us would like to forget. Not with the carbonometer. Linked to an emissions gauge in the exhaust system, the dashboard tally rises with every pump of the pedal, a stern reminder of the true cost of your quick trip to the supermarket.

Thou shalt give good weight.
Thou shalt not gouge.
Thou shalt not poach another designer's ideas nor do work
on spec.

Over the past several years, professional design associations
across the world have been drafting codes of ethics for their
members. But is this the best they can do? Lists of rules about
fees and decorum?

There is a need for ethical standards, sure. But in this planetary
endgame we now find ourselves in, ethics must take a much
longer view. Here's a more honest and straightforward code: the
code of true cost design.

true cost design

A client asks you to design a leaf blower. The little two-stroke engine you plan to use probably
has a life of a few thousand hours. Each one of those hours will produce a bit of stress and
annoyance and pollution for everyone who is forced to listen to the engine and to breathe its
fumes. And it will contribute to global warming. So before you start designing, you do the math.
You calculate how much that aggravation, pollution and climate change costs. For the sake of
this argument, let's say it costs ten cents per hour. You multiply that by the 3000-hour life span
of this tool. The result is a rough estimate of the ecological and psychological cost of your blower
over its lifetime: $300.

Now you have a decision to make. Is $300 per blower too high a price for society to pay? Can
you design a blower that is quieter, cleaner and less polluting? Should you turn down the job? Or
can you talk the client into designing a line of better rakes or leaf composters?

Of course, at the moment this whole exercise is highly subjective. In most cases we do not
have concrete criteria for calculating the social cost of the products we design. But this does
not mean we can give up and walk away. We must learn how to calculate these costs . . . bit by
bit, product by product, we must to turn what is now a theoretical exercise into something more
scientific and precise. If we don't, we will continue to be a destructive profession that calculates
these costs as zero, doing great potential harm with every product we create.

We designers are in a unique position – design being so new – of shaping our professional
culture as it grows. We can carve out a soul for it beyond the current commercial masturbation.
True cost is something we can pioneer, develop and live by, explain to our kids, put into our code
of ethics. It is something we can hang our profession on.

you teach the world to share

In the tradition of the kibbutz, the public library and the city bus, the design-to-share philosophy asks individuals to think globally, act neighbourly. Consider, for example, a neighbourhood toolshed, with workable innovations like a digital passcode, coin-op power tools, web-based reservations, and a community messaging system. Suddenly, something as humble as the common garden shed has transformed the way the whole community works.

Seven people waiting for the bus, sitting in a row and gently rocking in unison.

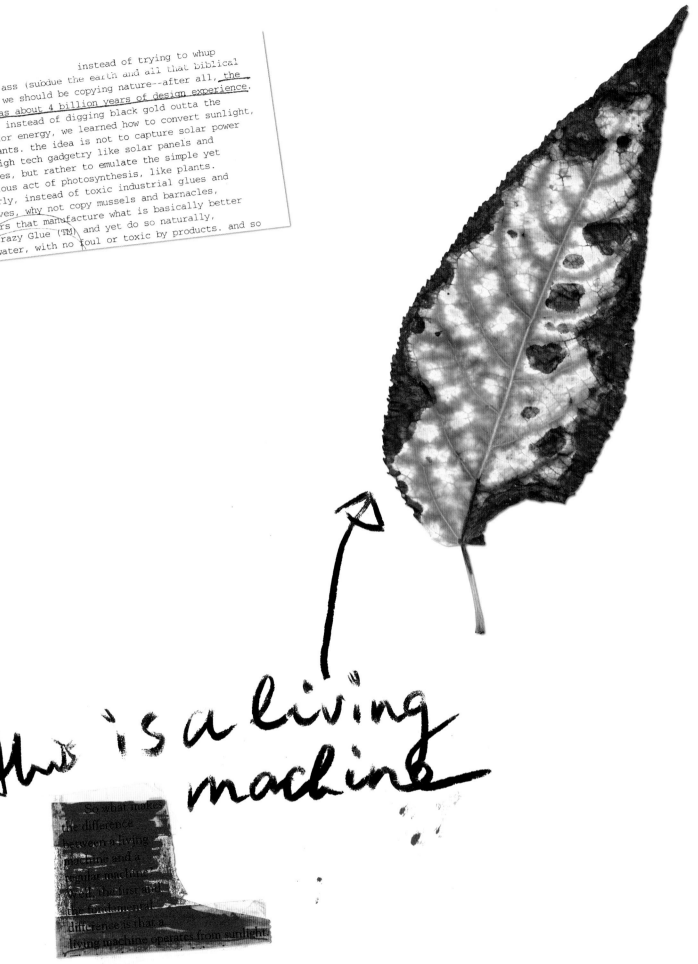

instead of trying to whup nature's ass (subdue the earth and all that biblical schtick) we should be copying nature--after all, the planet has about 4 billion years of design experience. what if, instead of digging black gold outta the ground for energy, we learned how to convert sunlight, like plants. the idea is not to capture solar power using high tech gadgetry like solar panels and batteries, but rather to emulate the simple yet mysterious act of photosynthesis, like plants. similarly, instead of toxic industrial glues and adhesives, why not copy mussels and barnacles, critters that manufacture what is basically better than Crazy Glue (TM) and yet do so naturally, underwater, with no foul or toxic by products. and so on.

this is a living machine

So what makes the difference between a living machine and a regular machine? well, the first and the fundamental difference is that a living machine operates from sunlight.

this is a living planet

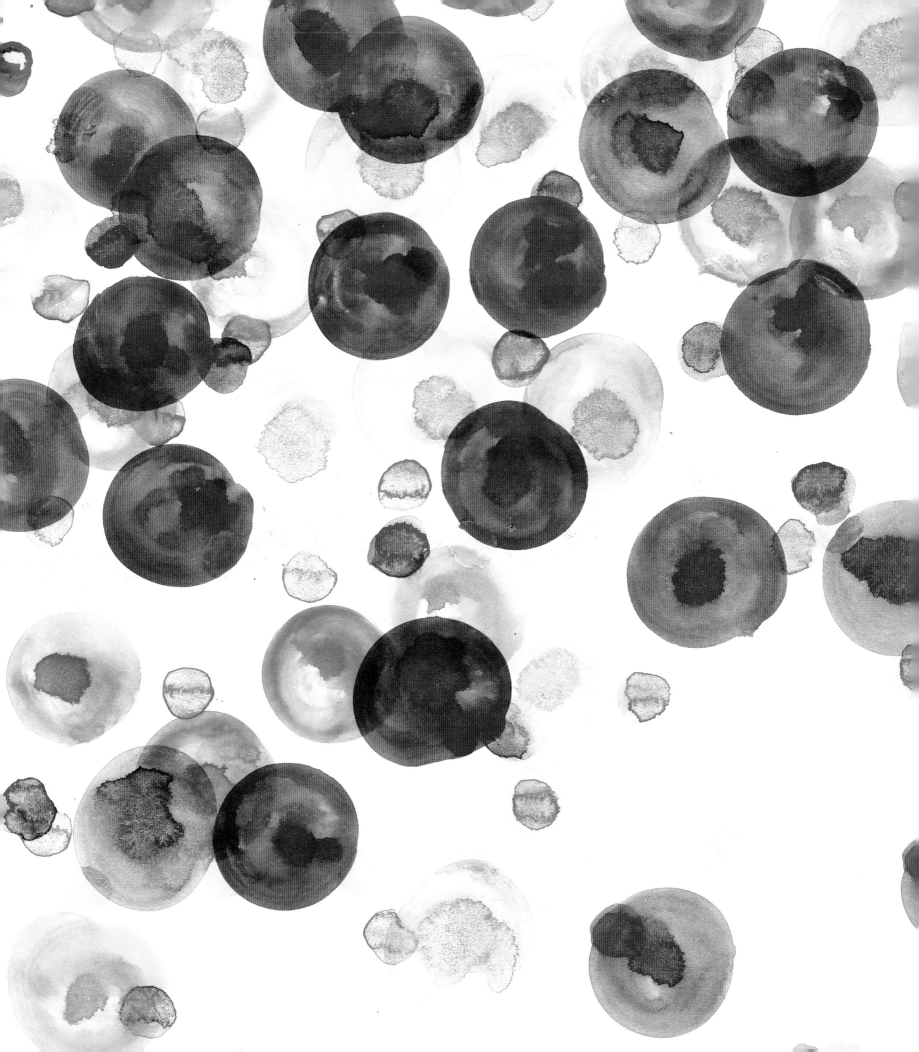

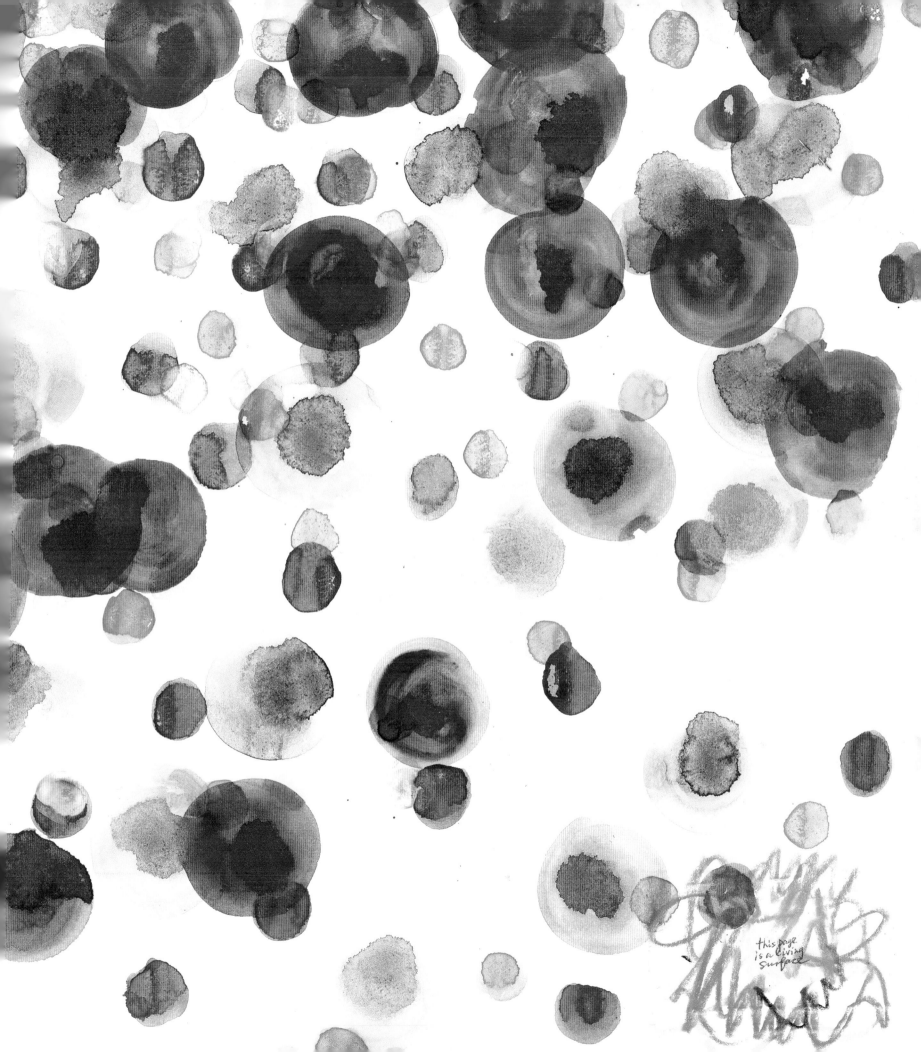

this page
is a living
surface

god is one.

> From: Lynne Elvins
> Subject: A reflection on teaching design students
> To: Kalle Lasn
>
> I teach young design students about using their talents in more 'sustainable' ways. These are people who
> after completing their degrees want to work for the 'cool and sexy' brand-name companies. We review
> the history of sustainable development, discuss the impacts of materials and impending legislation that
> will require recycling and reductions in hazardous materials for some product sectors. We also talk about
> branding and whether designers have a responsibility to bring about social improvement rather than just
> helping to sell stuff.
>
> When we start on what is usually an eight-week journey, the knowledge within the groups is mixed. One
> or two have usually already been exposed to the ideas, but have never connected their political agenda to
> what they do as designers. The majority think I will speak with them about recycling glass bottles at home,
> air pollution and deforestation. When I don't take this track, they are often pleasantly intrigued by what we
> discuss. Another minority vehemently reject what they see as a pointless hippy agenda and wonder why
> they are being made to learn this stuff.
>
> Recently, I had one such student respond strongly to the discussion on building accessibility into websites.
> The notion that he should "compromise" his design work for "a few blind people" seemed ridiculous to him,
> both creatively and financially. I suggested that if we wish to live in a society where people with disabilities
> -- not just blind people -- have the right to equal access, then surely they should have the right to experience
> his website. "I agree that buildings should be accessible," he replied, "but why should I change my design?
> I didn't make them blind." I was speechless at that point.
>
> Less dramatic, but far more endemic is the idea that things cannot change. Using the First Things First
> manifesto as a starting point, I ask all the students to argue both for and against its principles. The
> conclusions have been consistent for the past few years: "It's a nice idea, but it just won't work." The reason
> is often money: "It would be ok if everyone worked like this, but if I took this route now I wouldn't get a job."
> They have a point. More worrying is the response to whether it is a designer's job to give clients visionary
> solutions, to use design as a means to make life better. "No," is the majority view, "design is a commercial
> tool. We are not artists."
>
> After a few weeks there is often a new group within the class that are enjoying flexing their brains. They start
> to ask more questions and voice frustration. After viewing an advertisement for sustainable consumption
> made by Greenpeace, the students ask why they haven't seen this before: "It should be on TV. It would really
> help people understand." After I explain that its anti-buying sentiment would not be allowed on commercial
> TV, they are bemused: "That doesn't seem fair."
>
> Interestingly though, some students don't need teachers like me to offer them a different perspective on
> design; the industry appears to be putting people off all by itself. As I packed up at the end of last term,
> a few students came into the room to set up for the next presentation. They were studying 'branding and
> advertising' and were about to graduate later that year. "So, will you be aiming to join an in-house branding
> team" I asked them. "No", they replied, "from what we've learnt, it seems to us that branding and advertising
> is just shallow and pointless. We've decided we don't want anything to do with it anymore."

we design ourselves
out of a terrifying future

PROMETHEUS'
HOLY FIRE
IS IN MY
HANDS

Keep away
from children.

The perspective – the aesthetic – of our sustainable future has yet to take hold. But we can speculate. It's an honest, simple way of being. It follows organic cycles and mimics nature's ways. It's not so much about being moral or "good" as being a little bit wild and fiercely determined, like crabgrass growing through cracks in the concrete. It's about "being" rather than "having" and "process" rather than "form." As this new way of experiencing the world seeps into our imaginations, it begins to change our clothes, our houses, our shops, streets, food, music

a struggle for the imagination of the world

Meaning Is

Arbitrary And Without

FOUNDATION.

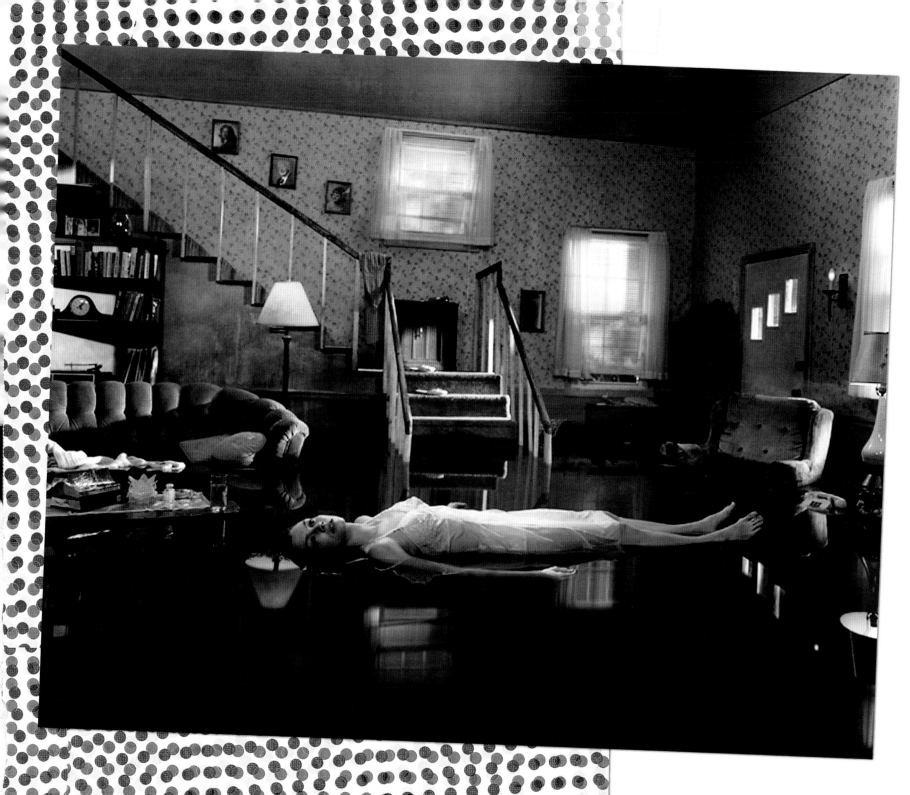

The *Weltan-schauung* has shifted from Platonic absolutism to a more relativist position,

To Impose a single text on readers is authoritarian AND oppressive

Making texts visually ambiguous and difficult to FATHOM is a way of respecting our readers.

Pete McCracken 'Erosive' 1993 GRISTY p242	**EROSIVE**	
	665	
Dave Henderickson 'Pulsitalia' 1994 GRISTY p242	**PULSITALIA**	
	666	
Pete McCracken 'Neo Deko' 1993 GRISTY p242	**NeoDeko**	
	667	
Scott Yoshinaga 'Grunge' 1993 GRISTY p242	**Grunge**	
	668	

So Let's lay obstacles, diversions and false trails.

EVERY GENERATION HAS ITS HEROES.
THIS ONE IS NO DIFFERENT.

MARXISM

modernism

feminism

Environmentalism

postmodernism

TERRORISM

the beginnings of sorrow

Let's halt and disrupt
the discourse

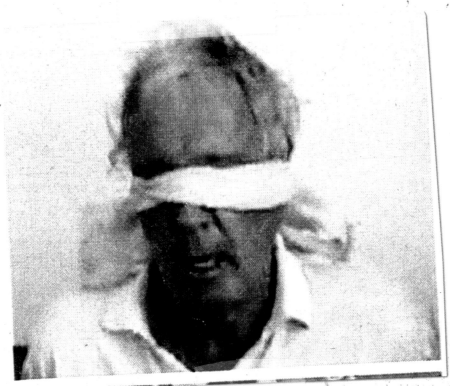

IN VARIOUS WAYS

"Terror is the ultimate spectacle for a tired, jaded populace.
— Don Delillo

Let's make movies so **big & loud** TV SO **FAST & FURIOUS** sometimes the viewer will feel **sick to their stomach**

but that's an appropriate reaction to much of the

20TH CENTURY.

ISN'T IT?

Chinese characters written in blood on the side of a bus. Muxidi, 4 June. (J. Annells)

But what if this SUBTERFUGE, IRONY, and DISRUPTION is just another bag of tricks?

a grand deception?

A free, authentic life is no longer possible. A continuous product message has woven itself into the very fabric of your life.

JUST YOU

and your friends

PICKING

around in the

hall of mirrors?

Lorem ipsum dolor sit amet, consetetur sadipscing elitr, sed diam nonumy eirmod tempor invidunt ut labore et dolore magna aliquyam erat, sed diam voluptua. At vero eos et accusam et justo duo

{ AFRAID
TO TAKE A STAND }

INS

C OMM

MM

HE

Are you losing your thirst for bubbly, brown, sugar water?

We go to corporations on our knees. Please do the right thing, we plead. Please don't cut down any more ancient forests. Please don't pollute any more lakes and rivers (but please don't move your factories and jobs offshore either). Please don't use pornographic images to sell fashion to my kids. Please don't pay governments off against each other to get a better deal. We've spent so much time bowed down in deference, we've forgotten how to stand up straight.

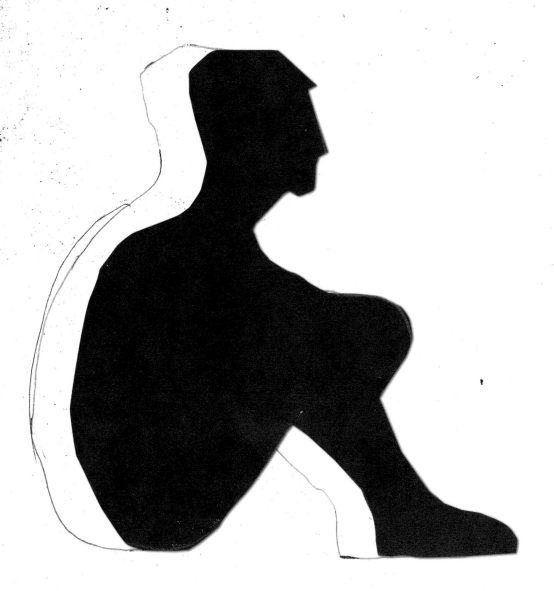

CHAPTER 9

We are ready to revitalize the argumentative and
confrontational traditions of design. We are ready to
move from the margins to centre stage in the ethical,
ecological and political debates of our time.

CULTURAL REVOLUTION IS OUR BUSINESS

We are a global network of artists, writers, environmentalists, teachers, downshifters, fair traders, rabble-rousers, shit-disturbers, incorrigibles and malcontents. We are anarchists, guerrilla tacticians, meme warriors, neo-Luddites, pranksters, poets, philosophers and punks. Our aim is to topple existing power structures and change the way we live in the twenty-first century. We will change the way information flows, the way institutions wield power, the way the food, fashion, car, and culture industries set their agendas. Above all, we will change the way we interact with the mass media and the way in which meaning is produced in our society.

Somos una red global de artistas, escritores, ambientalistas, profesores y empresarios, simplistas, desmadrosos, agitadores, incorrigibles e inconformistas. Somos anarquistas, tácticos de guerrilla, neo-ludistas, bromistas, poetas, filósofos y punks. Nuestra metas es derrocar las estructuras de poder existentes y cambiar la forma en que vivimos en el Siglo XXI. Cambiaremos la forma en que fluye la información, la forma en que las instituciones ejercen poder, y la forma en que las industries de la comida, la moda, el automóvil y la cultura establecen su orden del día. Sobre todo, cambiaremos la forma en que interactuamos con los medios masivos de comunicación, y recobraremos la manera en que se genera el propósito de nestra sociedad.

Nous sommes un réseau libre d'artistes, d'écrivains, d'écologistes, d'enseignants et d'entrepreneurs, de partisans d'une vie moins matérialiste, de semeurs de merde du secondaire, d'incorrigibles et d'insatisfaits. Nous sommes des anarchistes, de stratèges de guérilla, des nouveaux Luddites, des farceurs, des poètes, des philosophes et des punks. Nous visons à faire basculer les structures de pouvoir existantes et de changer comment nous vivons dans le 21ème siècle. On va changer le trajet de l'information, l'exercice du pouvoir dans les institutions, la manière dont les industries programment l'alimentation, la mode, l'automobile et la culture. Et par-dessus tout, on va changer notre relation avec les médias ainsi que la façon dont la signification se crée dans notre société.

Adbusters, even in its name, sets itself up as a resistance community, seeking to discredit and devalue consumerist culture and corporate rule. Because of this, they appeal to nearly all oppositional political groups, from environmentalists and anti-globalization activists to anti-tobacco activists and disillusioned corporate executives. Yet, as a coalition force, they fall into the typical coalition predicament (as seen with the recent anti-war movement) of being vehemently anti-something, but not pro-anything.

Moreover, the values from which Adbusters' anti-corporate feelings emerge as differend, are generally indescribable within the dominant logic of capital. Perhaps, as Bordieu describes, even their cognitive ability to resist is limited by established political frameworks. Their spoof commercials and mock advertisements tend to create self-fulfilling narratives that reinforce the dominance of the economic genre and the power of media. Potential seems to lie in subverting the system through decentered, localized actions such as their legislative initiatives (though potentially reformist) and direct actions against consumer culture. Yet, these cannot and will not succeed until they are accompanied, time and time again, by a precisely outlined set of values, meanings, and alternative ways of seeing and talking about the world. Whether such a language can be articulated is the essential question of modern oppositional politics.

From "The Politics of Language in Social Movements of the Information Age," a case study by Rob Levy.

Marlboro Country.

1992

"Now that I'm gone, I tell you: Don't smoke, whatever you do, just don't smoke."

— *Yul Brynner, in a television spot aired after his death from lung cancer in 1985*

If it wasn't for cigarettes, I wouldn't have cancer.

Warning: The Surgeon General Has Determined That Cigarette Smoking Is Dangerous to Your Health.

1976

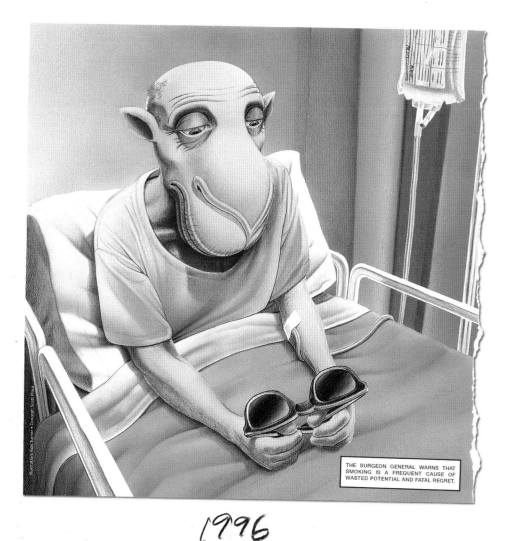

THE SURGEON GENERAL WARNS THAT SMOKING IS A FREQUENT CAUSE OF WASTED POTENTIAL AND FATAL REGRET.

1996

When they first appeared, the anti-smoking ads were so virulent, so stunningly truthful, so scary that it seemed like only a matter of time before they absolutely demolished the multi-billion dollar might of Big Tobacco.

I remember the ads vividly – close-ups of the glowing tips of cigarettes, X-rays of cruddy lungs. I remember Yul Brynner, whose last creative act in the world, after a slow disintegration from lung cancer, was to come on TV just months from death to look the world squarely in the eye. That meme forged the link between cigarettes and death. Everybody watching knew it was the truth. Those anti-ads helped me and millions of others to quit smoking. More significantly, they demonstrated that even a multinational cartel can be beaten in a free marketplace of ideas.

The anti-smoking meme crushed the smoking meme. Even with all of it's financial might, the tobacco industry was simply unable to compete because it lost its psychological stranglehold on the public mind. It lost its magic. Smoking was uncooled, and no amount of PR money could buy the cool back. Today a new generation of media activists are inspired by that victory. If the mighty tobacco industry was vulnerable to a calculated, tactical assault by small number of dedicated activists, then surely such subversive efforts can be repeated with success on other dysfunctional industries.

Altria

we will not allow a killer corporation to hide behind this blur

I miss my lung, Bob.

California Department Of Health Services.
Funded By The Tobacco Tax Initiative.

©1998 California Department of Health Services

1998

ABSOLUT IMPOTENCE.

DRINK "PROVOKES THE DESIRE BUT TAKES AWAY THE PERFORMANCE" — WILLIAM SHAKESPEARE

The ABSOLUT NONSENSE ad on the back cover of *Adbusters #5* set the tone for an all-out Absolut ad-spoofing craze: "Any suggestion that our advertising campaign has contributed to alcoholism, drunk driving or wife and child beating is absolute nonsense. No one pays any attention to advertising." Designers and artists from all over the world sent in their own spoofs. High school teachers challenged their students to come up with some. We started receiving fat wads of them in the mail, many of which we ran in the magazine.

Then Absolut tried to pour cold vodka on us. They sent us a cease and desist letter, demanding that we nix the spoofs, apologize for the damage done to their brand and destroy all remaining copies of the offending issues. So we put out a press release challenging them to a public debate about the value of alcohol advertising, and asking them why teenagers see thousands of alcohol ads before they reach the legal drinking age. When newspapers across North America began to pick up on our challenge, Absolut's international team of lawyers suddenly lost the nerve. We never heard from them again.

This little skirmish with Absolut left me grinning from ear to ear, my faith that it was possible to whip a big corporation in PR combat reaffirmed. In retrospect, though, I'm left wondering if it made any real, material difference. It's not as if Absolut's sales have plummeted, or as if alcohol ads are any less ubiquitous. And the fact that Absolut ad aficionados collect our spoofs alongside the official Absolut ads suggests a frightening prospect: a bottle-shaped void that stands ready to be filled with any meaning whatsoever – a cultural sponge, capable of absorbing every possible aesthetic, every possible movement, and every possible opposition.

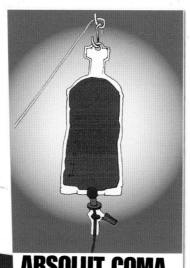

ABSOLUT COMA.

ABSOLUT MORON

ABSOLUTION?

ABSOLUTE MAYHEM

ABSOLUTE HANGOVER.

ABSOLUTE SILENCE.

ABSOLUT A.A.

ABSOLUTE ON ICE.

Our first assault against McDonald's appeared on the cover of *Adbusters #6*, with the fast-food giant's eponymous clown muzzled by a cheery little sticker that simply read "GREASE." Inside the issue, we offered instructions for a D.I.Y. version, and in no time the stickers were making appearances in McDonald's restaurants – pasted on windows, on food trays, and on cash registers.

OBESE

EAT FAST, DIE YOUNG

does this hit you in the gut?

The reason that activists so readily took up our humble little sticker was because we weren't exactly the only group targeting the multinational burger monger. From all quarters, McDonald's was coming under fire for the dubious nutritional value of its menu, for its exploitation of children as pliant marketing targets, for undercutting wages in the food service industry, and for generally contributing to the homogenization of global culture. For many activists, the public relations catastrophe that was the McLibel trials became the first glimmer of hope. When McDonald's posted it's first ever losses in 2003, after being forced to close more than 700 restaurants worldwide, victory seemed tantalizingly possible.

Fast forward a few years. McDonald's is once again chugging along nicely, now pushing yogourts and salads alongside the requisite burgers and fries – a slight triumph for nutritionists, perhaps, but cold comfort for the majority of McDonald's opponents. And McDonald's swift turnaround raises a disturbing question: Did all of our clever protests, all of our brilliant jams, our complaints and our devious pranks, did they ultimately just teach McDonald's how to market more effectively?

Do you want fries with that?
McCruelty to go.

PeTA 1-888-VEG-FOOD • MeatStinks.com

For so much of the twentieth century, the wide, uninterrupted stretch of pavement (whether freeway, highway, boulevard, or ring road) had come to represent a kind of freedom – the freedom of movement, the freedom of speed, the power of the internal combustion engine. Then things changed. Sometime in the early '90s, people began to turn against the streets.

Was it one too many traffic jams? One too many smog warnings? Public uproar over bulldozed neighbourhoods? Or foreign policy debacles in pursuit of more cheap oil to burn? Whatever the cause, people found themselves shaken out of the car-culture reverie, awakened to the degree that our cities had been given over to motor vehicles and to commercial convenience, usually at the expense of the livability and healthiness of the city itself.

In London, a grassroots protest over the construction of an intrusive highway grew into an unfamiliar form of direct action. The Reclaim the Streets movement, as it came to be known, began occupying roadways and city streets with spectacular and colourful parties, their simple though radical goal being to return human life to the asphalt. At around the same time, a group of San Franciscan cyclists, skateboarders, and rollerbladers embarked on the first ever Critical Mass, another form of street-takeover that focused on non-polluting forms of transportation. Rallying around the slogan "We aren't blocking traffic – we *are* traffic," they began to argue that if cars are unsustainable, then our cities should not be designed to accommodate them above all else.

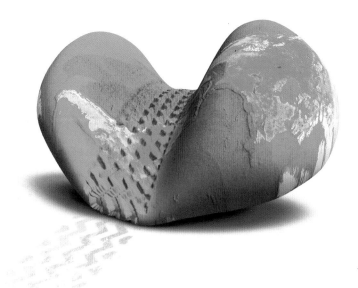

What was that bump?

Slow them, block them, walk right over them.

Alongside other public-space movements like guerilla gardening, both Reclaim the Streets and Critical Mass would swiftly become global social phenomena, a testament to the readiness of people all over the world to strive for workable alternatives to the car-centric, paved city.

By some measures, the push to rethink our cities and how we get around within them has been a massive success. Car-free days, pedestrian malls and other public transport initiatives have been institutionalized the world over as cities desperately search for ways to improve air quality and reduce infrastructure costs. Yet, it may be the case that the larger message about sustainability, about personal restraint, about human-scale development has been lost in the mad dash to meet woefully insufficient emissions goals and to dodge skyrocketing gas prices.

How to erode car culture:
— When it's not clear who has the right of way then YOU take the right of way; bit by bit we pedestrians win the battle of nerves with cars

WORLD CAR--FREE DAYS

www.adbusters.org
www.carbusters.ecn.cz

MAIDEN

We don't need another hero

AN ...TWORK BY BARB... ...IN CONJUNCTION WITH THE ILLUMINATIONS/CHA... ...'STATE OF THE ART'
PRE... ...E ...ANGEL TRUST W... ...CIAL ASSISTANCE FROM THE ARTS COUNCIL OF GR... ...INFORMATION PHONE...

Feed   Me

career

The extreme excesses of the beauty and fashion industries have long made them a particularly tempting target for culture jammers and art activists. By the mid-'90s a whole host of activists had successfully organized themselves around what are now familiar grievances: the sexual objectification of women; the mental-health consequences of being constantly exposed to unrealistic, even unattainable standards of beauty; and the pervasive exploitation of personal insecurities to assure a steady stream of profit for those who peddle beauty.

For many old-timers, the degree to which these grievances managed to saturate popular culture was astounding, though not necessarily heartening. The reason for this discontent? In the process of being taken up into commercial discourse, their far-reaching criticisms had mutated into a sort of unthreatening, soft-soap feminism, largely used to move more product. To some, it was a bittersweet victory; to others, it was a bitter defeat. But whether the glass is half full or half empty, in the present culture of unprecedented sexual commodification, you would be hard-pressed to argue that the cult of beauty has lost much of its steam.

Calvin Kline

OBSESSION

sisters

for women

"Only the vigilant can maintain their liberties, and only those who are constantly and intelligently on the spot can hope to govern themselves effectively by democratic procedures. A society, most of whose members spend a great deal of their time not on the spot, not here and now in the calculable future, but somewhere else, in the irrelevant other worlds of sport and soap opera, of mythology and metaphysical fantasy, will find it hard to resist the encroachments of those who would manipulate and control it."

—Huxley

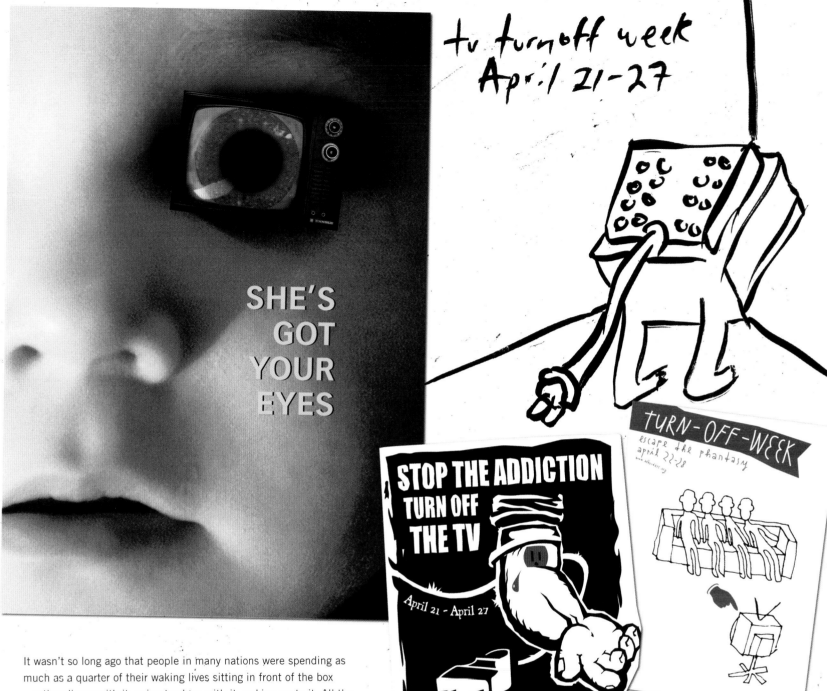

SHE'S GOT YOUR EYES

tv turnoff week
April 21-27

STOP THE ADDICTION TURN OFF THE TV

April 21 - April 27

TURN-OFF-WEEK
escape the phantasm
april 22-28

It wasn't so long ago that people in many nations were spending as much as a quarter of their waking lives sitting in front of the box – eating dinner with it, going to sleep with it, waking up to it. All the jokes about "couch potatoes" and "idiot boxes" disguised a grave truth, one that few people were willing to say aloud: our collective intimacy with television had grown into a full-fledged psychological dependency, the damaging effects of which were becoming painfully apparent.

Things changed drastically by the turn of the century. The allure of television – which many feared invulnerable – had been abruptly compromised. Mainstream support for TV Turnoff Week became widespread, and across a number of demographics TV viewership had actually fallen. At the same time, however, the amount of time spent staring at computer screens, playing video games, and using cell phones rose dramatically. TV may have been dethroned, but the throne has swiftly found some new tenants. Today the electronic environment dominates, and, for many, any connection with nature and local community has been all but severed.

THE MORE YOU CONSUME

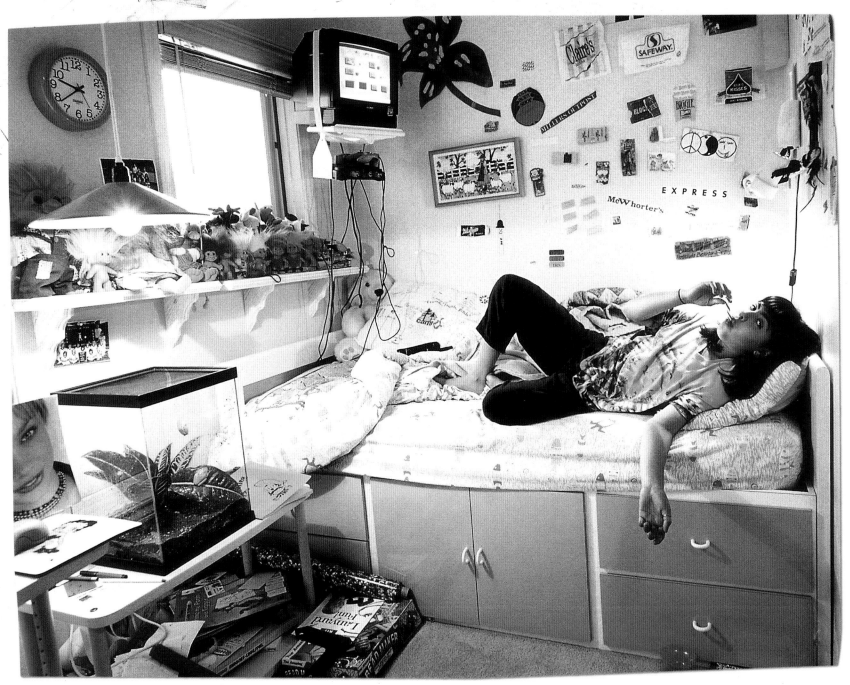

THE LESS YOU LIVE

1492 200102

I WANT YOU TO CURB YOUR CON$UMPTION THANKS!

WWW.ADBUSTERS.ORG

A 24 hour moratorium on consumer spending

BUY NOTHING DAY

JOURNÉE SANS ACHAT

26 NOVEMBRE 1999

CASSEURS DE PUB

antipub.net

לא קניות
BUY NOTHING DAY
בנובמבר 26

DIA SEM COMPRAS

24 שעות על תרבות הקניות,
הצריכה והאמריקניזציה!

26 DE NOVEMBRO DE 1999
WWW.ADBUSTERS.ORG

It was Vancouver artist/designer/activist Ted Dave who, back in 1992, first uttered the words "Buy Nothing Day." *Adbusters* had been struggling to come up with a nice, meaty concept for an anti-consumption campaign, and the moment we heard Ted's idea, we knew that we'd found it. Those three magic words would spread like wildfire, launching *Adbusters'* most successful social marketing campaign to date, a campaign that would in many ways come to be synonymous with the magazine.

The strength of Buy Nothing Day, its heart, is that it feels good. There's something deeply satisfying about making a promise to yourself and being able to stick to it, even if it's just for 24 hours. And even if you fail, you've learned something pretty profound about yourself — namely, that going cold turkey on shopping can be more of a struggle than you bargained for, a true battle of the will. In this sense, stepping out of the consumer stream can be a fascinating personal experiment. Will there be withdrawal, anxiety, an epiphany? Can you live without your cup of coffee or your Mars bar? Just how dependent on these little extravagances has your lifestyle become? Although BND is still young, people from all over the world have told of strange and wondrous realizations when they close their wallets and ditch spending for a day.

BND really found its footing in 1997, when we changed the date to the last Friday of November — the day after Thanksgiving in the US, a day that for many years has played host to the biggest shopping frenzy of the year, a day of crazy discounts and totally unrestrained bargain-hunting. Suddenly, BND took on a deeply cultural, almost spiritual significance. For US activists, it was the perfect opportunity to breed cognitive dissonance in the malls and big-box stores.

With the help of the Internet, BND participants began to orchestrate more and more elaborate pranks and public actions, then sharing their successes and failures with other activists from all over. At the same time, we discovered that designers and artists, both dabblers and professionals, were making huge contributions to BND in the form of posters, handbills, subvertisements, stickers, T-shirts — clever, hilarious, beautiful and shocking designs that would prove capable of tickling consumers and disarming opposition. By 2000, BND was being celebrated with gusto in over 65 countries, with credit card cutups, zombie invasions, and choreographed shopping-cart dances in malls, markets and high streets across the globe.

12345 67890

Participation in Buy Nothing Day has been driven mostly by the twin realization that overconsumption is the mother of all our environmental woes and that the relentless stream of ads and commercial messages that foster overconsumption are in turn degrading our collective mental environment. In the wake of several horrific acts of international terrorism, however, BND has also taken on a clearer geopolitical dimension. Could the hatred that fuels the attacks have anything to do with the staggering inequalities of the global economic system, a system that allows a minority of the world's citizens to gobble up the vast majority of the world's resources, leaving the rest to scratch at a very slender piece of the pie? Could this systemic disparity be one of the root causes of this ill-defined conflict in which we all find ourselves implicated? And, most tantalizingly, could a dose of Buy Nothing-style self-restraint offer one way out of the political, ecological and psychological quicksand?

The 200 or so corporations that were operating in the US by the year 1800 were each kept on a fairly short leash. They weren't allowed to participate in the political process. They couldn't buy stock in other corporations. And if one of them acted improperly, the consequences were severe. In 1832, President Andrew Jackson vetoed a motion to extend the charter of the corrupt and tyrannical Second Bank of the United States, and was widely applauded for doing so. That same year the state of Pennsylvania revoked the charters of ten banks for operating contrary to the public interest. Even the enormous industry trusts, formed to protect member corporations from external competitors and provide barriers to entry, eventually proved no match for the state. By the mid-1800s, antitrust legislation was widely in place.

The shift began in the last third of the nineteenth century – the start of a great period of struggle between corporations and civil society. The turning point was the American Civil War. Corporations made huge profits from procurement contracts and took advantage of the disorder and corruption of the times to buy legislatures, judges and even presidents. Corporations become the masters and keepers of business. President Abraham Lincoln foresaw terrible trouble. Shortly before his death, he warned, "Corporations have been enthroned . . . An era of corruption in high places will follow and the money power will endeavor to prolong its reign by working on the prejudices of the people . . . until wealth is aggregated in a few hands . . . and the republic is destroyed.

Lincoln's warning went unheeded. Corporations continued to gain power and influence. They had the laws governing their creation amended. Charters could no longer be revoked. Corporate profits could no longer be limited. Corporate economic activity could be restrained only by the courts, and in hundreds of cases judges granted corporations minor legal victories, conceding rights and privileges they did not have before.

We the People

Then came a legal event that would not be understood for decades (and remains baffling even today), and that would even change the course of American history. In Santa Clara County v. Southern Pacific Railroad, a dispute over a rail bed route, the US Supreme Court deemed that a private corporation was a "natural person" under the US Constitution and therefore entitled to protection under the Bill of Rights. Suddenly, corporations enjoyed all of the rights and sovereignty previously enjoyed only by the people, including the right of free speech.

A corporation has no heart, no soul, no morals. It cannot feel pain. You cannot argue with it. That's because a corporation is not a living thing, but a process – an efficient way of generating revenue. It takes energy from outside (capital, labour, raw materials) and transforms it in various ways. In order to continue "living" it needs to meet only one condition: its income must equal its expenditures over the long term. As long as it does that, it can exist indefinitely.

When a corporation hurts people or damages the environment, it will feel no sorrow or remorse because it is intrinsically unable to do so. (It may sometimes apologize, but that's no remorse – that's public relations.) Buddhist scholar David Loy, of Tokyo's Bunkyo University, put it this way: "A corporation cannot laugh or cry; it cannot enjoy the world or suffer with it. Most of all a corporation cannot love." That's because corporations are legal fictions. Their "bodies" are just judicial constructs, and that, according to Loy, is why they are so dangerous. "They are essentially ungrounded to the Earth and its creatures, to the pleasures and responsibilities that derive from being manifestations of the Earth." Corporations are in the most literal and chilling sense "dispassionate."

The unofficial history of America is not a story of rugged individualism and heroic personal sacrifice in the pursuit of a dream. It is a story of democracy derailed, of a revolutionary spirit suppressed, and of once-proud people reduced to servitude.

The engine behind *Adbusters* – the one thing that has always kept us going – is the David-and-Goliath joy of taking on the big guys. There is a moment of total exhilaration that comes when an apparently bullet-proof target reveals itself to be vulnerable – when Absolut Vodka backs down from a hysterical cease-and-desist order, or when a simple stickering campaign effectively shuts down McDonald's PR department for a week. After 15 years, though, the space between these moments seems to get longer and longer with each new campaign.

The biggest problem facing the design anarchist is the problem of recuperation, the nagging suspicion that each criticism and every protest ultimately serves to help dysfunctional corporations and opaque governments to improve their PR and fine-tune their marketing strategies. It is something with which the early avant-gardes struggled, with which the Situationists struggled as the '60s drew to a close, and with which culture jammers and art activists continue to struggle. The problem now is more intractable than ever.

Is it still possible to do anything outside of the capitalist model? Has the human spirit been tamed to the point that no opposition can escape being transformed into a marketing aesthetic? Has activism become nothing more than an amusing sideshow to the consumer capitalist circus?

CHAPTER 10

WORLD WAR IV
WILL BE FOUGHT
INSIDE YOUR HEAD

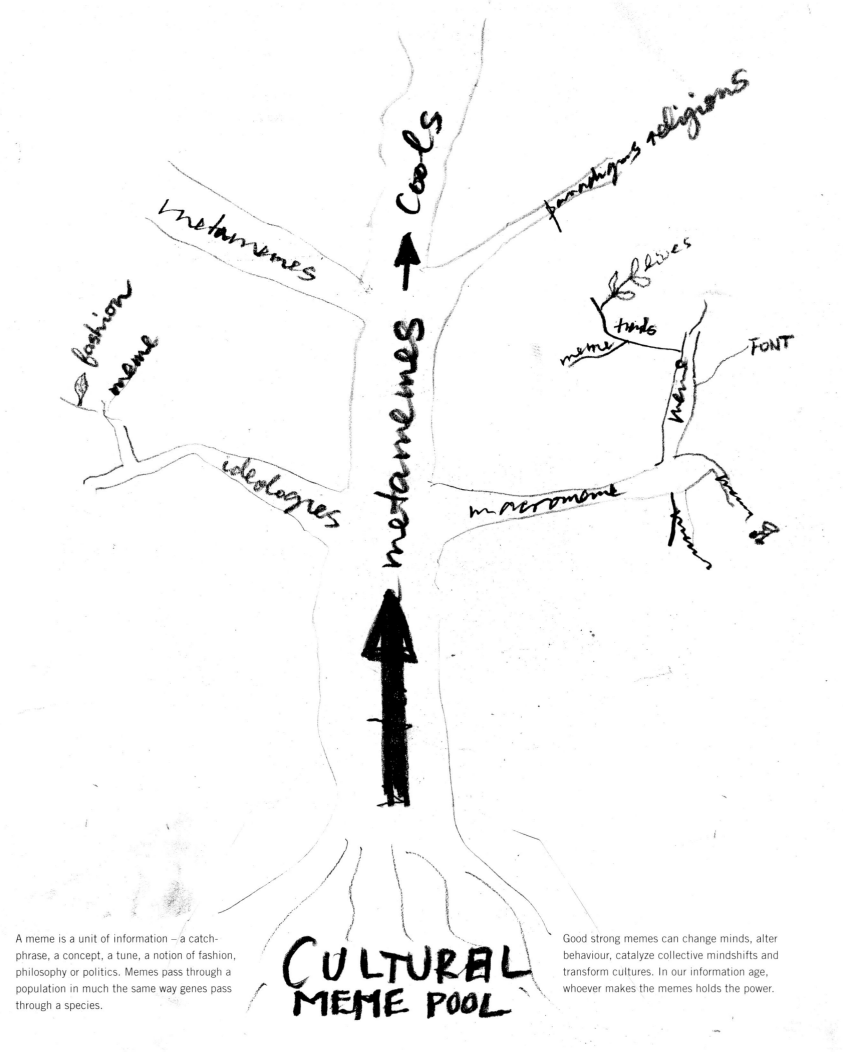

A meme is a unit of information – a catch-phrase, a concept, a tune, a notion of fashion, philosophy or politics. Memes pass through a population in much the same way genes pass through a species.

CULTURAL MEME POOL

Good strong memes can change minds, alter behaviour, catalyze collective mindshifts and transform cultures. In our information age, whoever makes the memes holds the power.

The next revolution – World War IV – will be, as Marshall McLuhan predicted, "a guerilla information war" fought not in the sky, nor on the streets, nor in the forests, nor around international fishing boundaries on the high seas, nor even on the battlefields of the Middle East, but rather in newspapers and in magazines, on the radio, on TV and on the Internet. It will be a dirty, no-holds-barred propaganda war of competing worldviews and religions and alternative visions of the future.

Meme Warfare

Corporations control much of the means of meme propagation, and they wield that power to devastating effect, foisting a few thousand ads, logos, marketing concepts and political slivers into our brains each day. In a sense, however, it all boils down to a single message: "You must consume." This message has altered everything, from the foods we eat, to how we get around, to the way we love and the way we lust, to how we frame the big issues that surround us. The question now is whether or not civil society can build its own meme factory, put out a better product and beat the corporations at the game they've dominated for so long.

Guy Debord proposed *détournement* as a way for people to take back the spectacle that had kidnapped their lives. Literally a "turning around," *détournement* involved rerouting spectacular images, environments, ambiences and events to reverse or subvert their meaning, thus reclaiming them. With its limitless supply of ideas, ranging from rewriting the speech balloons of comic-strip characters, to altering the width of streets and the heights of buildings and the colours and shapes of doors and windows, to radically reinterpreting world events such as the 1965 Watts riots in Los Angeles, the *Internationale Situationniste* – the journal the Situationists published between 1958 and 1969 – was a sometimes profound, sometimes absurd laboratory of provocation and *détournement*. Once, Debord altered a famous drawing of Lenin by placing a bare-breasted woman on his forehead with the caption "The Universe Turns on the Tips of Breasts." Debord had his book *Mémoires* bound in heavy sandpaper so that when it was placed on the shelves of libraries, it would destroy other books. One famous *détournement* happened in the Notre Dame cathedral on Easter Sunday in 1950. With thousands of people watching, a Lettrist provocateur dressed as a Dominican monk slipped onto the altar and delivered a sermon accusing the Catholic Church of "the deadly diversion of the force of life in favour of an empty heaven," and then solemnly proclaimed that "God is dead." It was with this spirit of *détournement* that the Situationists invaded enemy territory and tried to "devalue the currency of the spectacle." And it was with this defiance that they intended to pull off a cultural revolution, "a gigantic turning around of the existing social world."

highly charged zones
of symbolic contention

uncooling

Almost a century ago, Mahatma Ghandi asked the people of India to boycott British salt and cloth, and instead to make their own. It was the beginning of the end for the British Empire. Can we borrow a page from the past and boycott the corporate capital system into submission?

It would have to be like no other boycott in history. We know that a company's most valuable – and vulnerable – asset is its brand image. We also know that a brand crisis can bring a company to its knees. So here's the big question: can uncooling be one way for civil society to bring recalcitrant corporations to heel? We'd have to politicize every purchase we make, constantly look for opportunities and take them, because our target is a powerful force that surrounds us all the time. It's called corporate cool.

First thousands, then millions of people would need to start living strategically, each of us coming up with our personal boycott strategy, our own bag of tricks. We would have to adjust our lifestyles in sometimes painful ways: learn to live without foods and drinks we've loved since we were kids; find local alternatives to brands we consume every day without a second thought; shut out corporations that we've dealt with for years.

Can we do this? Can we play cat and mouse games with megacorporations? Outwit and outmaneuver them? Can we get millions of people, simultaneously, to ditch or switch brands? Can we, in a nutshell, learn to live lives of spontaneous, playful resistance?

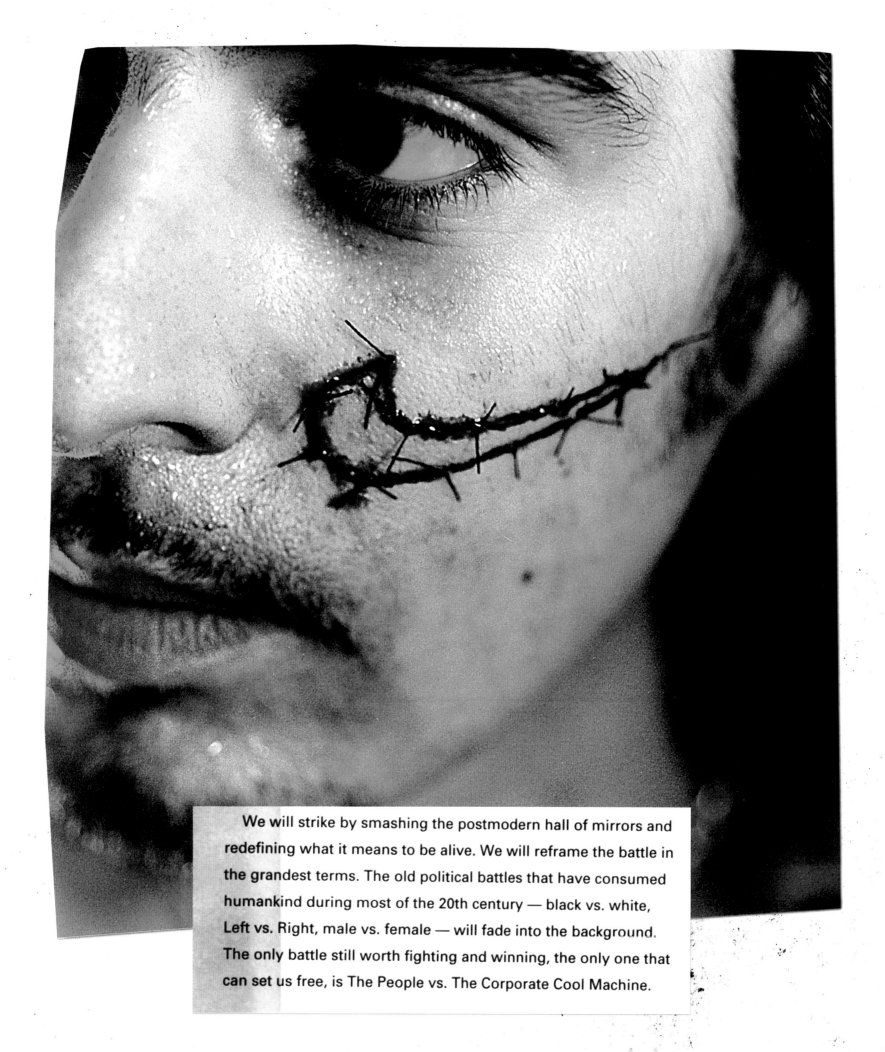

We will strike by smashing the postmodern hall of mirrors and redefining what it means to be alive. We will reframe the battle in the grandest terms. The old political battles that have consumed humankind during most of the 20th century — black vs. white, Left vs. Right, male vs. female — will fade into the background. The only battle still worth fighting and winning, the only one that can set us free, is The People vs. The Corporate Cool Machine.

YOU WALK INTO YOUR LOCAL TV STATION, PUT YOUR MONEY ON THE TABLE AND SAY, "GIVE ME 30 SECONDS OF AIR TIME."

Subvertising

30 secs

Design anarchists know how to get memes bubbling up in the public imagination. They produce stencils, posters, leaflets. They create newspaper and magazine ads and know how to raise the bucks to buy the space. But the 30-second TV spot – when well-conceived and well-produced by a team of passionate filmmakers – can turn into what I have long referred to as a "mindbomb," exploding in the collective psyche, sending out shock waves of fresh meaning. An effective TV subvertisement is so unlike that which surrounds it on commercial TV that it immediately seizes the viewer by the guts. It has the power to catch whole industries by surprise, to trigger government policy reviews, to derail legislation, to launch new political initiatives. It can shame the CEO of a corporation and trigger untold brand contamination. It is a legitimate way for a private citizen or activist group to challenge government, corporate, and industrial agendas. And the idea that you have the right to do that in a democracy is utterly empowering.

The average North American consumes five times more than a Mexican...

... ten times more than a Chinese person and thirty times more than a person in India.

We are the most voracious consumers in the world... a world that could die because of the way we North Americans live.

Give it a rest. November 26 is Buy Nothing Day.

BUY NOTHING DAY

PARTICIPATE BY NOT PARTICIPATING

POV. Hands holding fast-food tray.

VOICE OVER:
Did you know . . .

Hands bring Big Mac closer to camera.

VOICE OVER: . . . that 50% of·the calories from a Big Mac come · from fat?

Hands throw burger back down onto tray; sounds of disgust.

www.adbusters.org/videos

In an alternate universe where fair play reigns supreme, television is a vibrant and contentious zone. McDonald's chimes in as usual, touting its new double-the-meat Big Mac and pseudo-Asian grilled chicken salad. But then, without warning, and on strangely equal footing . . . something else entirely.

The Situationists were the first to realize what is happening to us, what it means to be sucked up by the spectacle. Now we're really in the spectacle, and the spectacle is really in us . . .

MOMMY....?

cognitive dissonance

Cognitive dissonance – a high-tension state between two opposing beliefs – is the design anarchist's most indispensable tool. It works like a pie in the face, first inducing confusion, then anger, and finally an intense desire to correct the imbalance – to rediscover the consonance that has been lost.

Cognitive dissonance is old hat in the marketing world, where it's used to manipulate people into making decisions that they wouldn't normally make. Take the classic foot-in-the-door technique, for example. You ask your mark for a tiny favour, or get him to answer in the affirmative to some innocuous question ("Do you ever worry about your children's safety?" or "Would you say that most people don't smile enough?"). Then you make your pitch. Since your mark has already said yes to you once, he finds it harder to refuse the pitch.

Design anarchists use cognitive dissonance in an entirely different and thoroughly less predictable way. They take a cherished or mundane image and turn it on its head – make it seem grotesque or repulsive or bizarre – and force people to radically reconsider what they hold dear and what they take for granted. Whether spread via a stickering campaign or a big-budget TV campaign, design dissonance provides the jolt that gets people making their own life-altering choices.

THE EVOLUTION OF MARKETING

Marketing: selling society on an ever-expanding horizon of products and services.

Social Marketing: selling society on a new set of ideas, lifestyles, philosophies and world views.

Negamarketing: urging society to consume less electricity, gasoline, energy, materials.

Demarketing: unselling the consumer society; turning the incredible power of marketing against itself.

15 secs

FEELING EMPTY?

DON'T WORRY

CONSUMPTION
WILL FILL THE VOID

"We don't want to take any advertising that's inimical to our legitimate business interests."
—NBC network commercial clearance manager Richard Gitter

I WAS LOOKING FOR A NEW WAY OF BEING

Once I started relating to the world as an empowered human being
instead of a hapless consumer drone, something remarkable happened.
My cynicism dissolved. My interior world suddenly became vivid. I felt
like a cat on the prowl: alive, alert, and still a little wild.

< adbusters.org >

The post-consumer generation will demand greater meaning in life – which might spell, if not an end, then a radical reorientation of consumer capitalism.

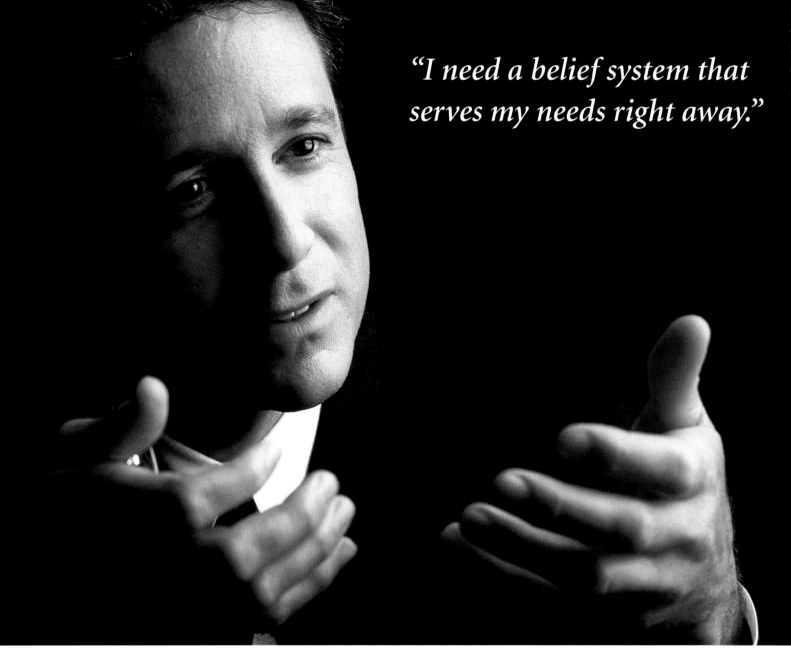

"*I need a belief system that serves my needs right away.*"

Dean Sachs has a mortgage, a family and an extremely demanding job. What he doesn't need is a religion that complicates his life with unreasonable ethical demands.

Spiritual providers in the past have required a huge amount of commitment — single-deity clauses, compulsary goodness, and a litany of mystifying mumbo-jumbo. It's no wonder people are switching to Mammon.

Mammon isn't the biggest player in the spiritual race. But our ability to deliver on our promises is unique. And our moral flexibility *unmatchable.*

MAMMON

Because you deserve to enjoy life – guilt free.

Americans seem to embrace withering critiques of the consumerist ethos such as this barb in Adbusters magazine, but they're not deterred by them from heading out to the mall.

BUY NOTHING DAY

We begin by demarketing ourselves, our lives, our bodies, our children's bodies. Then we join with others to demarket our chief social and cultural rituals, now warped beyond recognition by commercial forces. Mother's Day, Easter, Hallowe'en, Thanksgiving, Christmas – all can be reclaimed.

Zen Santa

ZACH, age 9
Loves: Sleeping, Survivor, Playstation. **Hates**: Teachers, my sister.
When I grow up I want to: Be a gangsta rapper.
If I was in charge of the world: I'd clean up the air and the oceans.
In 10 years there will be: A big war and the world will be a crazy mess.

A BILL OF RIGHTS FOR FUTURE GENERATIONS

WE, THE PEOPLE of the future, like the twenty thousand generations who came before us, have the right to breathe air that smells sweet, to drink water that runs pure and free, to swim in waters that teem with life, and to grow our food in rich, living earth.

We have the right to inherit a world unsullied by toxic chemicals, nuclear waste, or genetic pollution. We have the right to walk in untamed nature and to feel the awe that comes when we suddenly lock eyes with a wild beast.

We beseech you, the people of today: do not leave your dirty messes for us to clean up; do not take technological risks, however small, that may backfire catastrophically in times to come. Just as we respectfully ask that you not burden us with your deferred debts and depleted pension plans, we also claim our right to a share of the planet's ecological wealth. Please don't use it all up.

We, in turn, promise to do the same. We grant these same rights and privileges to the generations who will live after us; we do so in the sacred hope that the human spirit will live forever.

A curse on any generation who ignores this plea.

> Before economics can progress it must abandon its suicidal formalism.
> —*Robert Heilbroner*

Some intellectual paradigms are so insular, so incestuous and so thoroughly rigid that they will resist and suppress any and all calls for major change, regardless of the actual merit of those changes. But this resistance cannot be maintained forever. There comes a day when even the most hopelessly autistic of disciplines is overwhelmed by its own inadequacies, from every corner. When such a day comes, the discipline is recast in a cataclysmic blaze.

Neoclassical economics is one such paradigm. At this moment, small groups of economics students in a handful of influential universities are triggering visceral debate by calling for an end to the hermetic formalism of economic thought. They are calling for a whole new economics – a true-cost economics, a post-autistic economics, an ecological economics. And among the looming disappearance of petroleum, the collapse of supposedly renewable resources, and the devastatingly violent responses against global economic injustice, their voices are growing louder.

What other disciplines, other professions, other intellectual paradigms are similarly vulnerable to the sort of spectacular collapse that the world evidently has in store for neoclassical economics?

Kick It Over!

neoclassical economics

Before economics
can progress, it
must abandon its
suicidal formalism.
-*Robert Heilbroner*

REDEFINING PROGRESS

ADBUSTERS

ADBUST...

ENVIRONMENT

NO FUTURE

SEP/OCT 2004 · #55

No Future

US/CAN $7.95 · UK £4.00 · ¥1400

VOL. 12 · NO. 5 SEP/OCT 2004

TRUE COST ECONOMICS MANIFESTO

WE, THE UNDERSIGNED, make this accusation: that you, the teachers of neoclassical economics and the students that you graduate, have perpetuated a gigantic fraud upon the world.

You claim to work in a pure science of formula and law, but yours is a social science, with all the fragility and uncertainty that this entails. We accuse you of pretending to be what you are not.

You hide in your offices, protected by your jargon, while in the real world forests vanish, species perish, human lives are ruined and lost. We accuse you of gross negligence in the management of our planetary household.

You have known since its inception that your measure of economic progress, the Gross Domestic Product, is fundamentally flawed and incomplete, and yet you have allowed it to become a global standard, reported day by day in every form of media. We accuse you of recklessly supporting the illusion of progress at the expense of human and environmental health.

You have done great harm, but your time is coming to its close. The revolution of economics has begun, as hopeful and determined as any in our history. We will have our clash of paradigms, we will have our moment of truth, and out of each will come a new economics – open, holistic, human scale.

On campus after campus, we will chase you old goats out of power. Then, in the months and years that follow, we will begin the work of reprogramming the doomsday machine.

TRUECOSTECONOMICS.ORG

charter review

It won't be long before civil society once again has the means to control corporate conduct. We will begin with a survey of corporate charters, with every state, every province, every prefecture conducting public reviews of all the corporations under its jurisdiction. If a corporation has broken a law, or has hurt customers, employees or society, it can be reprimanded, fined or instructed to clean up its act by the next charter hearing.

charter revoke

When a corporation grievously misbehaves, when it is caught knowingly dumping toxic wastes, damaging watersheds, fixing prices or keeping vital information secret from customers, employees or shareholders, then that corporation may be legally "sentenced to death" – its charter is revoked, its assets sold off and the money funnelled into a superfund for its victims.

three strikes & you're out

Any corporation found guilty of betraying the public trust three times, even for less-than-horrific infractions, automatically has its charter revoked – no exceptions.

You attack the wrong-doer from above with hard-hitting media memes. You break its unchallenged run on television by airing dissenting ads. You run subverts and spoofs in magazines and on the web. You place countermemes right next to theirs, and watch them scramble to contain the fireworks.

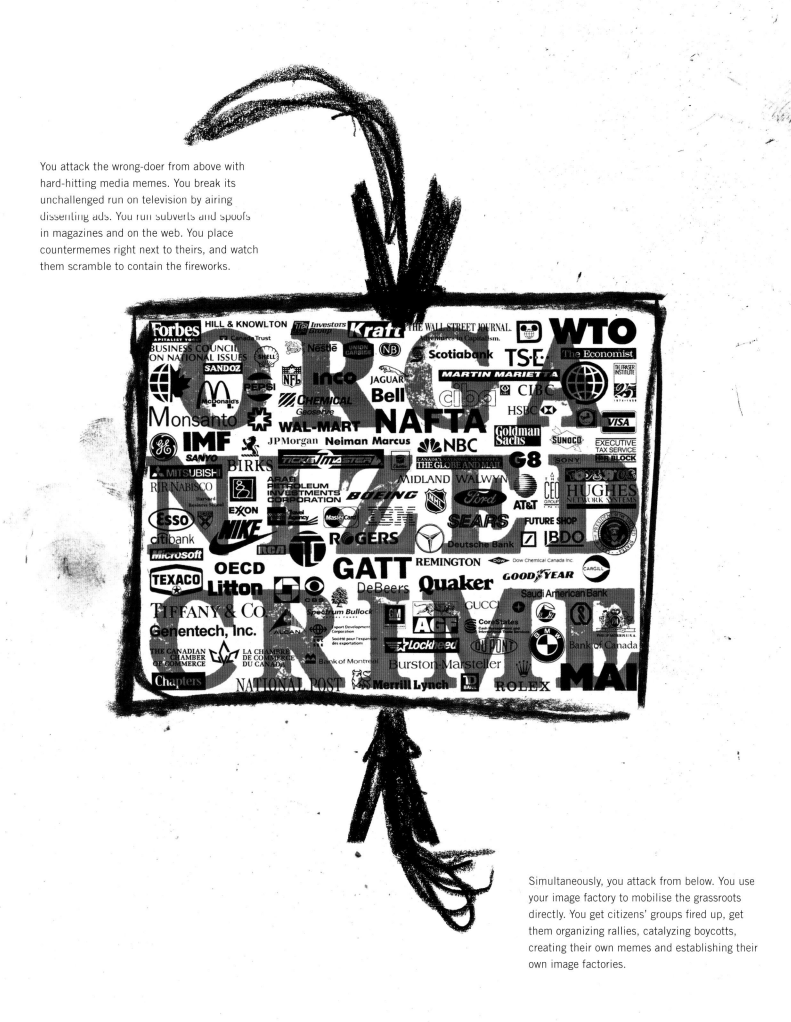

Simultaneously, you attack from below. You use your image factory to mobilise the grassroots directly. You get citizens' groups fired up, get them organizing rallies, catalyzing boycotts, creating their own memes and establishing their own image factories.

WHY MUST THIS VANDAL DEFACE MY LIBERAL UTOPIA?

vandalism

anarchists in a street protest. We seek to explore vandalism as an intentional mode of

aesthetic expression as it presents itself formally in its object, and as it relates to the social

conditions of our age. Adorno's demand for thoroughly self-conscious art might lead us to suspect that vandalism lacks the depth to adequately capture the realm of the subject, but what could be

a more complete expression of the desperate cynicism of post-modern decadence than the

cathartic, primal lashback at felt powerlessness? What more determinate aesthetic form

would not import some shred of false hope for an escape that did not involve a direct and

urgent confrontation with property, the precariously inflated value around which we have

built ourselves?

In May 1968, the Situationist-inspired Paris riots set off "a chain reaction of refusal" against consumer capitalism. First students, then workers, then professors, nurses, doctors, bus drivers and a piecemeal league of artists, anarchists and *Enragés* took to the streets, erected barricades, fought with police, occupied offices, factories, dockyards, railway depots, theatres and university campuses, sang songs, issued manifestos, sprayed slogans like "Live Without Dead Time" and "Down with the Spectacular-Commodity Culture" all over Paris, and challenged the established order of their time in the most visceral way. The breadth of the dissent was remarkable. "Art students demanded the realization of art; music students called for 'wild and ephemeral music'; footballers kicked out managers with the slogan 'football to the football players'; grave diggers occupied cemeteries; doctors, nurses, and the interns at a psychiatric hospital organized in solidarity with the inmates." For a few weeks, millions of people who had worked their whole lives in offices and factories broke from their daily routines and *lived*.

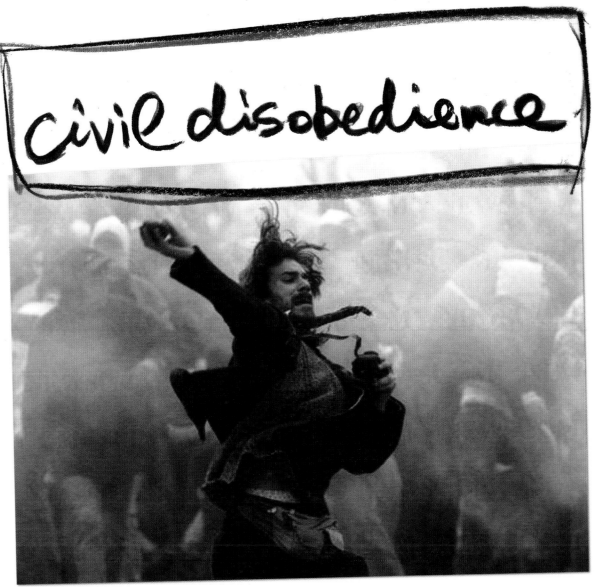

civil disobedience

We will raise the pitch of resistance to the point where airport-type security systems are needed just to let customers into stores, until the daily cost of doing business as usual becomes simply too high to bear.

abcdefghijklmn
opqrstuvwxyz

We kick in the rotten door and charge into the vacuum.

the quick brown fox jumps over the lazy dog

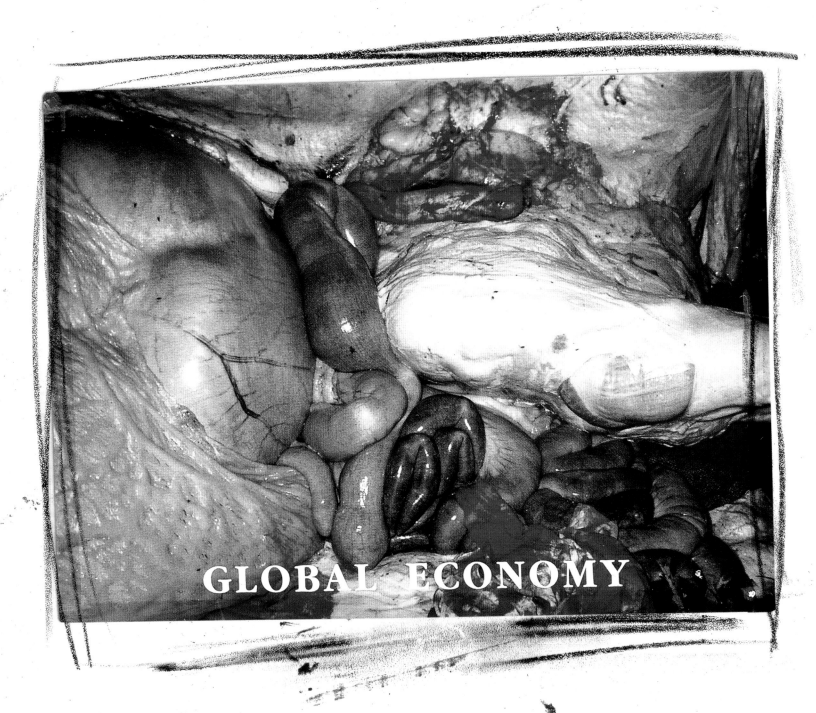

GLOBAL ECONOMY

It won't take too many of us – a global network of about 500 of us can pull this thing off. We start by brainstorming on the Internet. Through trial and error, wild ideas and incremental refinements, we create a steady stream of memes: stories, stickers, posters, flash animations, games, songs, documentaries, TV mindbombs, happenings, provocations and pranks that communicate the absurd, cold-blooded unsustainability of it all: the perversity of a system that thrives off the death of nature and the backs of future generations. We unleash wave after wave of cognitive dissonance, life-affirming epiphanies, devastating moments of truth. Meme by meme, mindbomb by mindbomb, protest by protest, we take the piss out of consumer capitalism and crystallize a new vision of the future – a new style and way of being – a sustainable agenda for planet Earth.

revolution is not showing life
to people but making them
live

GD

The American dream has devolved into exactly the kind of vacant obliviousness the Situationists talked about – a smile–button–have-a-nice-day kind of happiness that close examination tends to disturb. If you keep up appearances, keep yourself diverted with new acquisitions and constant entertainments, keep yourself pharmacologized and recoil the moment you feel real life seeping in between the cracks, you'll be all right.

Some dream.

If the old American dream was about prosperity,
maybe the new one will be about spontaneity.

Design Anarchy is madness. Choose
it only if you're certain the other
options will corrode your soul and
give you a bleeding ulcer. Only if
you know you are among the chosen
few designers who hold Prometheus'
holy fire in your hands. You'll suffer
for years and live like a stray dog,
but you'll have the joy of breaking
all the rules, of freely mixing art
and politics, of pouring your beliefs
and convictions into your work.
Eventually, if you're really as brilliant
as you think, you'll have a crack at
pushing the boundaries of global
culture with bold new forms and
fresh ways of being.

eeeeeeeee eeeeeeeee eeeeeeeee

Beowolf (FontShop, 1990) is at root a statuesque text roman drawn by
Erik van Blokland. The letterforms are sent to the output device through
a subroutine, devised by Just van Rossum, that provokes distortions of
each letter within predetermined limits in unpredetermined ways. Three
degrees of randomization are available. Within the specified limits, every
letter is a surprise.

Make a promise to yourself: start living again . . . having fun
. . . kicking ass . . .

c. 1970
Designer unknown

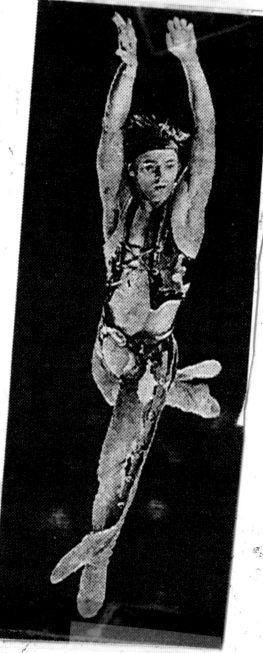

CHAPTER 11

Dancing when

you don't know

the next step

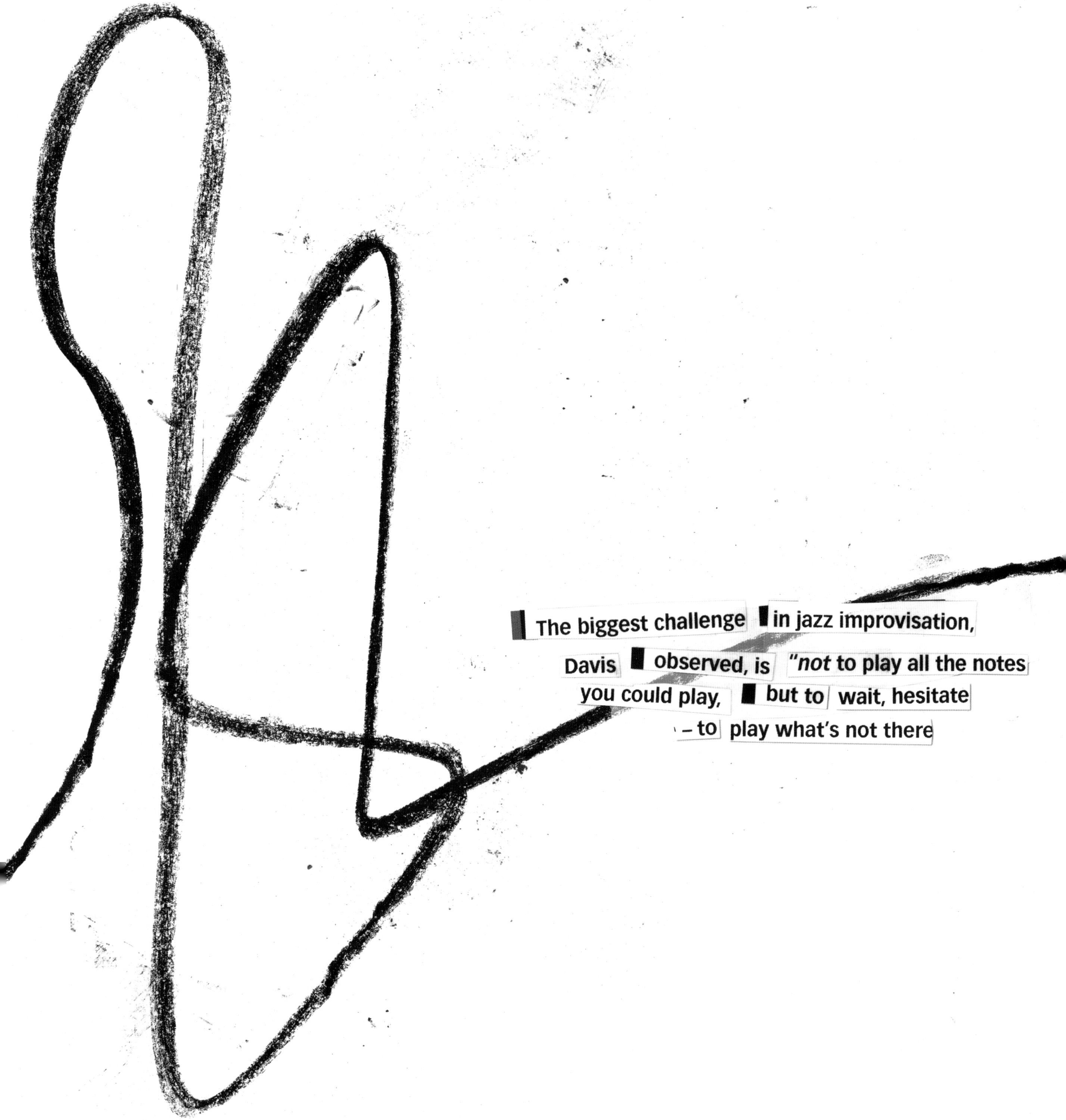

The biggest challenge in jazz improvisation, Davis observed, is "*not* to play all the notes you could play, but to wait, hesitate — to play what's not there

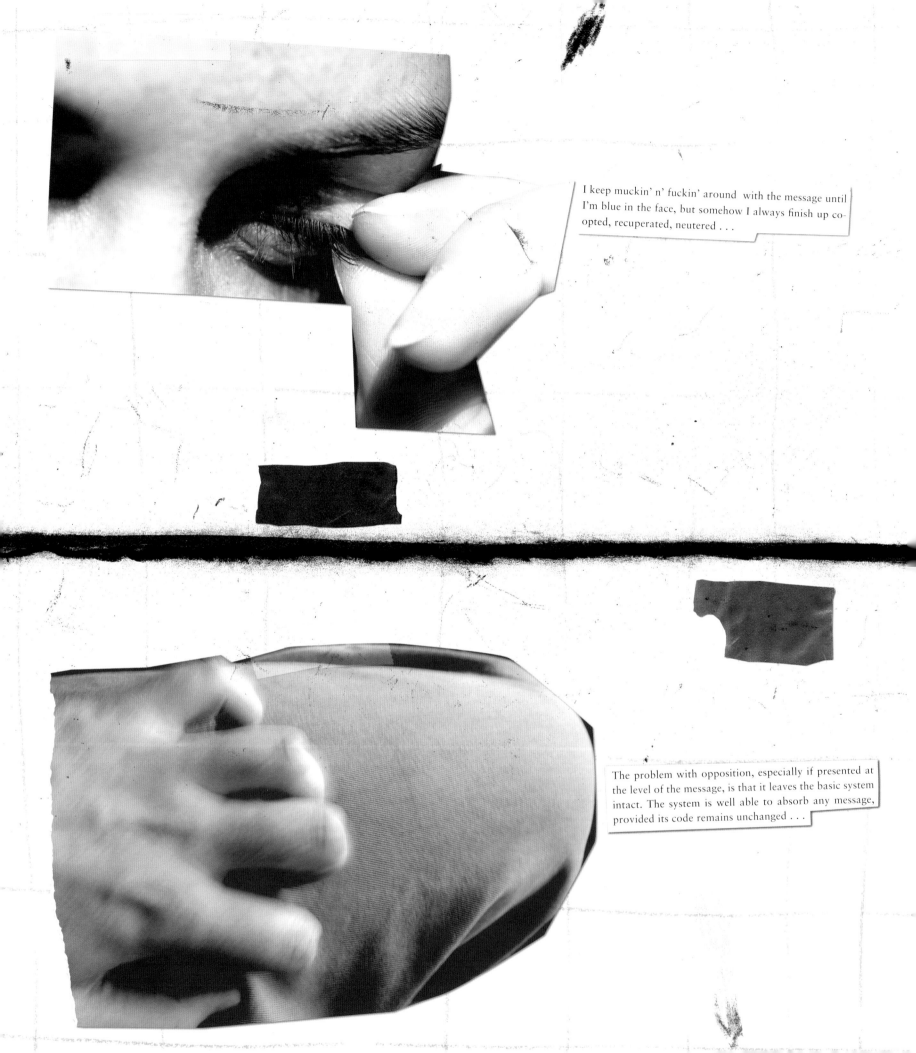

I keep muckin' n' fuckin' around with the message until I'm blue in the face, but somehow I always finish up co-opted, recuperated, neutered . . .

The problem with opposition, especially if presented at the level of the message, is that it leaves the basic system intact. The system is well able to absorb any message, provided its code remains unchanged . . .

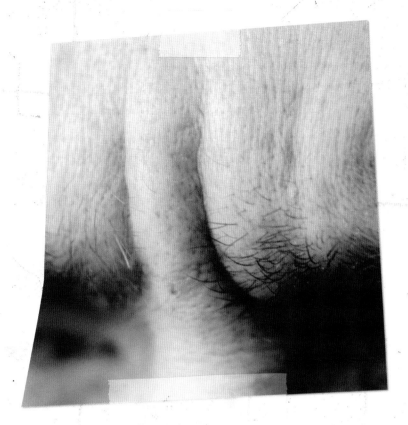

Joseph Beuys sounded crazy claiming he was going to change the world through his art. But his way of trying to change things was more metaphysical than the kind of easy manipulation of popular images that we're into today.

I heard a story about how David Hammons made snowballs of different sizes, then sold them on a Brooklyn street to passersby. Imagine how the experience of buying a snowball and then watching it slowly melt away would stay with a person . . . maybe even for the rest of your life.

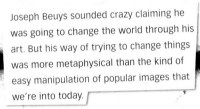

a sudden unexpected moment of truth

a rupture in
the normal practices

of politics and society
which destroys the
regime's monologue

we smash the hall of mirrors...

AD FREE ZONE
OUR SCHOOL

we break the   commercial monopoly on the production of meaning...

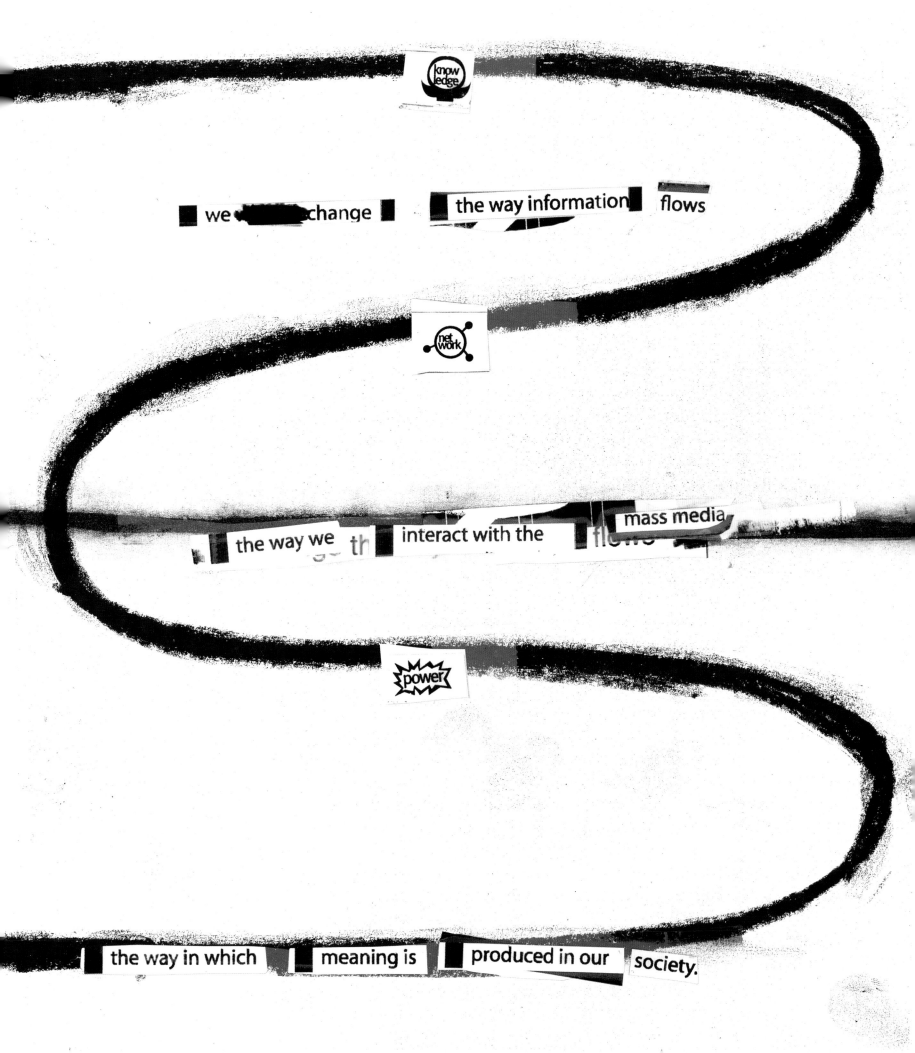

knowledge

we ▮▮▮▮ change   the way information   flows

network

the way we   th   interact with the   flows   mass media

power

the way in which   meaning is   produced in our   society.

- End of slavery
- Universal suffrage
- End of child labor
- Education rights
- Religious freedom
- Civil rights
- Women's rights
- Disabled people's rights
- Gay rights
- Environmental justice
- Animal rights
- Intergenerational rights
- Communication rights

MEDIA CARTA

WE, THE UNDERSIGNED, ARE TROUBLED BY THE WAY INFORMATION FLOWS AND THE WAY MEANING IS PRODUCED IN OUR SOCIETY.

WE HAVE LOST CONFIDENCE in what we are seeing, hearing and reading: too much infotainment and not enough news; too many outlets telling the same stories; too much commercialism and too much hype. Every day, this commercial information system distorts our view of the world.

WE HAVE LOST FAITH in the institutions of the mass media. A handful of corporations now control more than half the information networks around the world. At a time when people worldwide face hunger, social disruption, war and ecological collapse, only those who know how to walk the walk, talk the talk or pay big bucks are getting their message across.

WE HAVE LOST HOPE that our national media regulators will act in the public interest. Essential rules limiting media ownership and concentration are being scrapped, while rules protecting local content and access are diluted.

WE HAVE LOST PATIENCE waiting for reform.

WE IMAGINE A DIFFERENT SYSTEM — a media democracy. We see great promise in the open communications of the internet and want that openness expanded into every form of media. We envision a global system of communications that has as its foundation the direct, democratic participation of citizens. To this end, we demand the timely transfer of key media sources back to the people.

As a start, we demand the right to buy radio and television airtime under the same rules and conditions as advertising agencies. We ask our media regulators to set aside two minutes of every broadcast hour for citizen produced messages. We want the six largest media corporations in the world broken up into smaller units.

What we ultimately seek is a new human right for our information age, one that empowers freedom of speech with the right to access the media. This new human right is: The Right to Communicate.

WE HEREBY LAUNCH A MOVEMENT to enshrine The Right to Communicate in the constitutions of all free nations, and in the Universal Declaration of Human Rights.

WWW.MEDIACARTA.ORG

CHAPTER 12

The society that abolishes every
adventure makes its own abolition
the only possible adventure

one packet of sarin
one mad cow
one pinch of anthrax
one hand-held rocket launcher
one 10 cm sphere of plutonium

Doubtless, the present situation is highly discouraging. We have watched the war machine grow stronger and stronger, as in a science fiction story; we have seen it assign as its objective a peace still more terrifying than fascist death; we have seen it maintain or instigate the most terrible of local wars as parts of itself; we have seen it set its sights on a new type of enemy, no longer another State, or even another regime, but the "unspecified enemy"; we have seen it put its counterguerrilla elements into place, so that it can be caught by surprise once, but not twice. Yet the very conditions that make the State or World war machine possible, in other words, constant capital (resources and equipment) and human variable capital, continually recreate unexpected possibilities for counterattack, unforeseen initiatives determining revolutionary, popular, minority, mutant machines. —Badiou

Newspaper photograph depicting the victims of gang warfare or social cleansing in a Rio de Janeiro shantytown.
The killers reveal both their ethical and aesthetic sensibilities by carefully arranging the corpses for full effect.

Helvetica Ultra Light 14 points
Helvetica Thin 14 points
Helvetica Light 14 points
Helvetica Roman 14 points
Helvetica Medium 14 points
Helvetica Bold 14 points
Helvetica Heavy 14 points
Helvetica Black 14 points

OUR GEOPOLITICAL FUTURE

incessant technical renewal —
integrated spectacle —

~~the merging of state and economy~~

generalized secrecy —
unanswerable lies
an eternal present

— Guy Debord

TRIPLE WITCHING HOUR

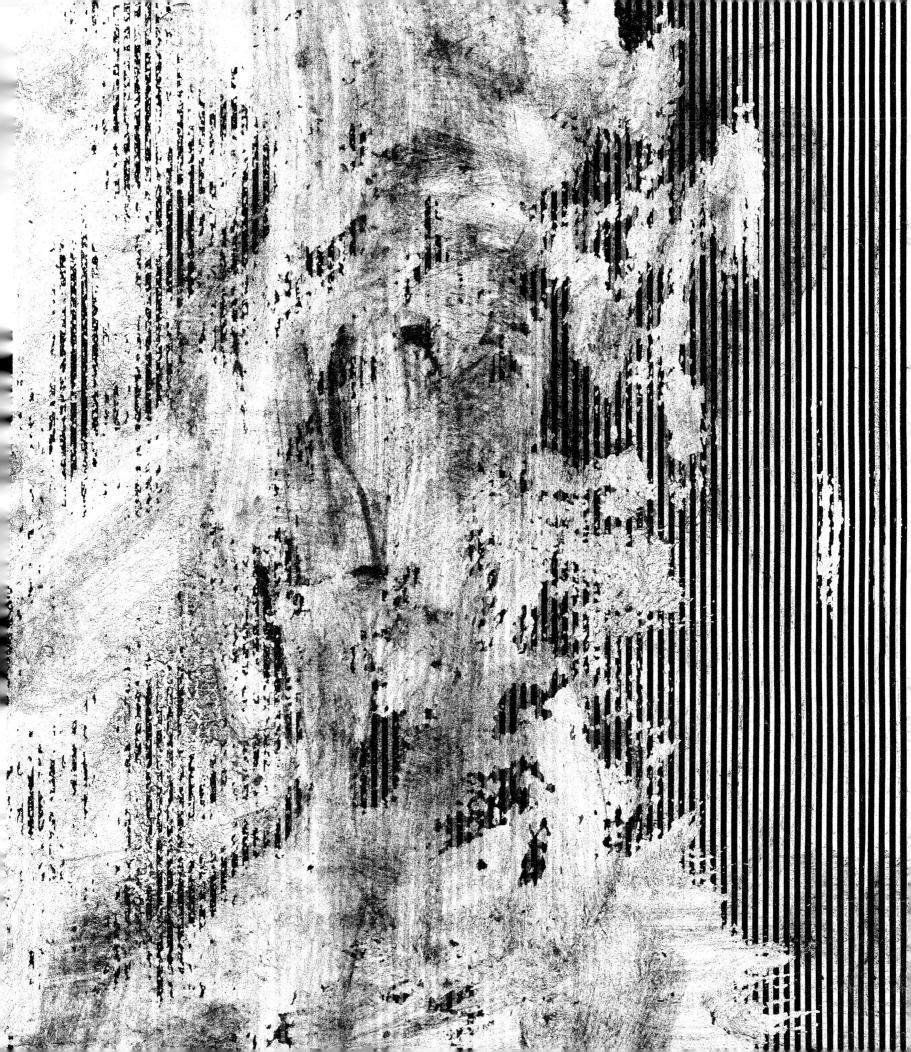

THE BEGINNINGS OF SORROW

EXHAUSTED

WHAT WENT WRONG?

Explanations for the collapse cannot be summed up in a single idea or one catastrophic event. The truth lies somewhere deeper down. What went wrong started going wrong a long time ago, perhaps as far back as the start of our evolution as human beings, certainly at the start of our own cultural evolution. Deep in the recesses of our minds and societies, there exist structures that govern our ways of thinking and being. These structures, built over centuries as a dialectic between inner mind and outer world, have a destructi... still remains hidden fro...

the death of God

free at last, free at last
from the tyranny of style

One day you'll be blind like me. You'll be sitting here, a speck in the void, in the dark, forever, like me.

One day you'll say to yourself, I'm tired, I'll sit down, and you'll go and sit down. Then you'll say, I'm hungry, I'll get up and get something to eat. But you won't get up. You'll say, I shouldn't have sat down, but since I have I'll sit on a little longer, then I'll get up and get something to eat. But you won't get up and you won't get anything to eat.

You'll look at the wall a while, then you'll say, I'll close my eyes, perhaps have a little sleep, after that I'll feel better, and you'll close them. And when you open them again there'll be no wall any more.

Infinite emptiness will be all around you, all the resurrected dead of all the ages wouldn't fill it, and there you'll be like a little bit of grit in the middle of the steppe.

Yes, one day you'll know what it is, you'll be like me, except that you won't have anyone with you, because you won't have had pity on anyone and because there won't be anyone left to have pity on you.

Samuel Beckett, *Endgame*

the end of history

the courage

(as a species)

to die

Gary
Snyder
"Turtle Island"

New Directions, 74

FOR THE CHILDREN

The rising hills, the slopes,
of statistics
lie before us.
the steep climb
of everything, going up,
up, as we all
go down.

In the next century
or the one beyond that,
they say,
are valleys, pastures,
we can meet there in peace
if we make it.

To climb these coming crests
one word to you, to
you and your children:

stay together
learn the flowers
go light

Time it takes to grow one inch of soil: 1,000 years

My sense of beauty changes as I approach death
now I like small rather than imposing things
colours that are not so bright
I like latent more than dynamic energy
understatement more than hyperbole
I relish the still moment before the action itself
and the other day
it dawned on me why Basho's only poem about Mt Fuji
describes a day when fog prevented him from seeing the peak...

quiet, stillness, and empty space
will be craved

416

Adbusters Media Foundation
1243 West 7th Avenue
Vancouver, British Columbia V6H 1B7
Canada

ISBN 0-9746800-9-5

Printed in China by ORO Editions.